www.wadsworth.com

wadsworth.com is the World Wide Web site for Wadsworth and is your direct source to dozens of online resources.

At *wadsworth.com* you can find out about supplements, demonstration software, and student resources. You can also send email to many of our authors and preview new publications and exciting new technologies.

wadsworth.com
Changing the way the world learns®

SEVENTH EDITION

Writing Papers in Psychology

A STUDENT GUIDE TO RESEARCH REPORTS, LITERATURE REVIEWS, PROPOSALS, POSTERS, AND HANDOUTS

Ralph L. Rosnow and Mimi Rosnow

THOMSON
WADSWORTH

Australia • Canada • Mexico • Singapore • Spain
United Kingdom • United States

THOMSON
━━━━✦━━━━ ™
WADSWORTH

Publisher: Victoria J. Knight
Editorial Assistant: Monica Sarmiento
Technology Project Manager: Erik Fortier
Marketing Manager: Dory Schaeffer
Marketing Assistant: Nicole Morion
Advertising Project Manager:
 Brian Chaffee
Project Manager, Editorial Production:
 Candace Chen
Art Director: Vernon Boes
Print Buyer: Doreen Suruki

Permissions Editor: Kiely Sisk
Production Service: Robin Gold, Forbes
 Mill Press
Copy Editor: Margaret Ritchie
Illustrator: International Typesetting
 and Composition
Cover Designer: Roger Knox
Cover Image: © Masterfile Corporation
Cover and Text Printer: Webcom
Compositor: International Typesetting
 and Composition

Printed in Canada
1 2 3 4 5 6 7 09 08 07 06 05

For more information about our products,
contact us at:
**Thomson Learning Academic Resource
Center
1-800-423-0563**
For permission to use material from this
text or product, submit a request online at
http://www.thomsonrights.com.
Any additional questions about
permissions can be submitted
by email to
thomsonrights@thomson.com.

Library of Congress Control Number:
2004117063

ISBN 0-534-53331-0

**Thomson Higher Education
10 Davis Drive
Belmont, CA 94002-3098
USA**

Asia (including India)
Thomson Learning
5 Shenton Way
#01-01 UIC Building
Singapore 068808

Australia/New Zealand
Thomson Learning Australia
102 Dodds Street
Southbank, Victoria 3006
Australia

Canada
Thomson Nelson
1120 Birchmount Road
Toronto, Ontario M1K 5G4
Canada

UK/Europe/Middle East/Africa
Thomson Learning
High Holborn House
50–51 Bedford Row
London WC1R 4LR
United Kingdom

To the partnership
that brought this book about

and

to Miles, R.J., Sasha, and Matthew
whose promise shines

About the Authors

Ralph L. Rosnow is Thaddeus Bolton Professor Emeritus at Temple University in Philadelphia, Pennsylvania, and has also taught communication research at Boston University and social psychology and research methods at Harvard University. **Mimi Rosnow** has done freelance editorial consulting and for a number of years was an editorial assistant at a national magazine.

Brief Contents

Contents

CHAPTER SEVEN **Writing and Polishing** 73

CHAPTER EIGHT **Producing the Final Manuscript** 93

CHAPTER NINE **Crafting a Poster
and a Concise Report** 114

Exhibits

Preface for Instructors

This seventh edition of *Writing Papers in Psychology* provides frameworks, tips, guidelines, and sample illustrations for college students who are writing research reports or literature reviews that are expected to conform to style recommendations in the fifth edition of the *Publication Manual of the American Psychological Association* (hereafter called the APA manual). Chapter One contains a flowchart (Exhibit 1) that walks the student through all phases of these two projects as well as the proposal and, if required, a poster and a concise summary of the research for distribution. *Writing Papers* is intended to be more than just an APA style guide, however. It is designed to cultivate skills in organizing, literature retrieval, critical reasoning, and communication under deadlines. For students who do not plan to continue in psychology, the APA style may have little relevance after the baccalaureate, but these other skills should be relevant for a lifetime.

Several instructors have told us they have used *Writing Papers* to usher their graduate students into the APA style. For students writing papers for submission to scholarly journals, and particularly for those planning to enter the academic writing and publishing world, we recommend reading Robert J. Sternberg's *The Psychologist's Companion* (Cambridge University Press, 1993) and Joseph M. Moxley's *Publish, Don't Perish* (Praeger, 1992). For those preparing meta-analytic reviews, two other essential references are Robert Rosenthal's "Writing Meta-Analytic Reviews" (*Psychological Bulletin*, 1995, *118*, 183–192) and Harris Cooper and Larry V. Hedges's *Handbook of Research Synthesis* (Russell Sage, 1994). For anyone preparing a PowerPoint presentation, Edward R. Tufte's *Cognitive Style of PowerPoint* (www.edwardtufte.com) is another source worth reading. Whether one is writing for a course or professionally, an essential style reference is Will Strunk and E. B. White's classic "little book," *Elements of Style* (Allyn & Bacon, 2000), a gem of a book that belongs on every author's desk.

New to This Edition

In 1999, the APA's Task Force on Statistical Inference examined the limitations of the rhetoric of the "accept/reject" paradigm in null hypothesis significance testing and recommended guidelines for reporting effect sizes and confidence intervals.[1] Although similar guidelines are reflected in the APA

---

[1] L. Wilkinson & Task Force on Statistical Inference. (1999). Statistical methods in psychology journals: Guidelines and explanations. *American Psychologist, 54,* 594–604.

manual, researchers have shown slowness in embracing them, which critics attribute to inertia as much as to incongruities in the APA manual.[2] Regarding the APA manual's recommendation that confidence intervals be reported for effect sizes involving principal outcomes, we explain the reasoning in a chapter new to this edition of *Writing Papers* (Chapter Six). Several texts in psychological statistics and research methods now describe how to calculate certain effect sizes and confidence intervals. In the new chapter, we list additional references for those seeking further guidance. In particular, the chapter emphasizes the importance of reporting statistical information clearly, accurately, precisely, and in enough detail to allow others to reach their own conclusions. An exhibit lists common statistical terms and their meanings, as a way of jogging the student's memory and demystifying the terms used in this chapter and the sample report.

Interspersed throughout the chapters are leit motif anecdotes that are intended to clarify and drive home key ideas and to make the technical details and guidelines more palatable. All the chapters and sample materials have been revised to some degree. Chapter Two has been substantially revised to reflect the rapid changes in literature retrieval. The emphasis is still on PsycINFO, the default database recommended by most psychology instructors, but new to this edition of *Writing Papers* is a free four-month subscription to InfoTrac® College Edition. InfoTrac provides full-text access to the *Annual Review of Psychology* and hundreds of journals in many fields. In Chapter One, we have added a typology of literature reviews, based on the work of Harris Cooper. In Chapter Three, we have expanded on the idea of replication, so that students have a clearer idea of what it means to "add an innovative aspect of one's own."

Recommended Style

There are some departures from the APA manual, as *Writing Papers* focuses on students' term papers and research reports for course assignments, whereas the APA manual is focused on the preparation of manuscripts for submission to journals. Instructors' needs may be different in some respects from journal editors' and reviewers' requirements. For example, many instructors of research courses like to see the raw data and the statistical calculations, so they can assess whether any mistakes are due to misunderstanding, carelessness, or typographical errors. An appendix to the sample research report contains this information.

Another departure from APA style is the cover page of the student's paper. There is, of course, no compelling reason to require a recommended

---

[2] F. Fidler (2002). The 5th edition of the APA publication manual: Why its statistics recommendations are so controversial. *Educational and Psychological Measurement, 62,* 749–770; F. Fidler, N. Thomason, G. Cumming, S. Finch, & J. Leeman. (2004). Editors can lead researchers to confidence intervals, but can't make them think: Statistical reform lessons from medicine. *Psychological Science, 15,* 119–126.

"running head" (the purpose of which is to suggest to the copyeditor an abbreviated title to be printed at the top of the pages of a published article), but there is a good reason to ask for a page header (to make it easier to get the pages back in order should they be scattered). Other information shown on the cover page is relevant to the course and the instructor.

Interestingly, the APA has for some time been flexible in some of its style requirements, as indicated on the old APA Publication Manual Web site (www.apa.org/journals/faq.html). For example, a student inquired whether the title shown on the title page of a manuscript belonged in the middle of the page or closer to the top of the page. The student had noticed that "colleagues' versions of the Publication Manual showed a different graphic for the title page of a manuscript." The APA response was that either version was correct. Another person, referring to the fourth edition of the APA manual, asked why underlining was required instead of italicizing, inasmuch as computers make it just as easy to italicize as to underline. The APA answered that underlining tells the typesetter to use italics, but that if a manuscript for publication is in final form, it is quite acceptable to use the italicizing function to mimic what would be typeset in italics and to improve the appearance of the manuscript. The standard in *Writing Papers* is to use italics, as recommended in the fifth edition of the APA manual.

Regarding the hanging versus paragraph-type indent for references, the APA manual has wavered back and forth in the third, fourth, and fifth editions. The APA's Web site response to a question was "If you are preparing a manuscript in final form, meaning that the manuscript will not later be typeset and published, you may prefer to format references with a hanging indent to enhance readability." The fifth edition of the APA manual recommends, but does not insist on, the hanging indent; the APA manual does caution, however, that "the chosen format should be consistent throughout the references" (p. 299). The sample materials in *Writing Papers* use the hanging-indent format for references.

In reporting quantitative values, students are often puzzled by how many decimal places to indicate. The APA manual's rule of thumb is to report descriptive data (e.g., means, standard deviations, Cohen's d) and inferential test results (e.g., t, F, chi-square) to two decimal places—the standard used in *Writing Papers*. In computing statistical results by hand, however, problems could arise if the student scrimped on the number of decimal places in the intermediate calculations, as rounding errors could produce inaccurate results. To emphasize this point, all of the intermediate calculations indicated in the appendix of "Jane Doe's" report (Appendix A) are not rounded to two decimal places (though scientific calculators and computers do not round until the end anyway).

Students also frequently ask how to report statistical significance, particularly when they see statements like "significant difference" and "no significant difference" but no indication of the actual p value. Statements like these can be terribly misleading if all the writer means is that the obtained p value was on the "wrong" side of .05. There is something absurd about regarding as a "real effect" one that is supported by $p = .05$ and as a "zero effect" one that is supported by $p = .06$. The sample research report shows the tabular values to two decimal places and shows the p values more precisely indicated in the results section (using scientific notation to compress the number of decimal places). Chapter Six provides further guidance while also cautioning students to avoid the traps of false precision and needless precision in reporting results.

Acknowledgments

We thank two outstanding psychology teachers, Anne A. Skleder (Alvernia College) and Bruce Rind (Temple University), for earlier versions of the sample papers, which we have reworked in different editions of *Writing Papers;* we especially thank Dr. Rind for the raw data in the research report, which are empirical data that he collected. We also thank another outstanding teacher, Eric K. Foster, for the literature retrieval experience launching Chapter Two ("Maya" is the name of Dr. Foster's daughter). We thank Bob Rosenthal for keen insights that helped us improve Chapter Six. We benefited from using reference resources at Temple University's Paley Library, especially the Web site created by Richard Lezenby. We thank Marion Harrell of the American Psychological Association for her suggestions for updates of our discussion of PsycINFO and its companion resources. We are grateful to Vicki Knight of Thomson Wadsworth for her interest and enthusiasm, to Ken King for encouraging us to get started on this book many years ago, and to James Brace-Thompson for his support of previous editions. Once again, we thank Margaret Ritchie for her skillful editing.

We thank the following reviewers and other colleagues, whose helpful suggestions have improved one or more editions of *Writing Papers:*

John B. Best, Eastern Illinois University
Thomas Brown, Utica College of Syracuse University
David E. Campbell, Humboldt State University
Scott D. Churchill, University of Dallas
Peter B. Crabb, Penn State University-Abington
Nicholas DiFonzo, Rochester Institute of Technology
Nancy Eldred, San Jose State University
Kenneth Elliott, University of Maine at Augusta
Eric K. Foster, Temple University
Robert Gallen, Georgetown College
David Goldstein, Duke University
John Hall, Texas Wesleyan University
Donald Hantula, Temple University
James W. Kalat, North Carolina State University
Allan J. Kimmel, Groupe École Supérieure de Commerce de Paris, France
Arlene Lundquist, Mount Union College
Joann Montepare, Tufts University

Quentin Newhouse, Jr., Bowie State University
Ben Newkirk, Grossmont College
Arthur Nonneman, Asbury College
Edgar O'Neal, Tulane University
Rick Pollack, Merrimack College
Maureen Powers, Vanderbilt University
MaryLu Rosenthal, Riverside, California
Robert Rosenthal, University of California at Riverside
Gordon W. Russell, University of Lethbridge, Canada
Helen Shoemaker, California State University at Hayward
John Sparrow, State University of New York at Geneseo
Claudia Stanny, University of West Florida
David B. Strohmetz, Monmouth University
Stephen A. Truhon, Winston-Salem State University
Lori Van Wallendael, University of North Carolina

Finally, we thank the many users of *Writing Papers*. Your suggestions have helped us to improve each new edition. We again invite instructors and students to send us recommendations for further improvements (http://rosnow. socialpsychology.org).

Ralph and Mimi Rosnow

1

GETTING STARTED

Writing papers to fulfill course requirements means knowing what the instructor expects and then formulating a plan to accomplish your goal on schedule. This chapter includes some simple dos and don'ts to help you avoid pitfalls and to ensure that the assignment will be completed on time and that it will represent your best work.

Where to Begin

There was once an intriguing character named Joe Gould, who, after graduating from Harvard in 1911 and trying his hand at a number of futile endeavors, moved to New York and began to hang around Greenwich Village coffee shops. He told people that he had mastered the language of seagulls and was translating literature into "seagull," and in fact, he did an uncanny imitation of one. He was best known, however, for an ambitious project he claimed to be compiling, called the "Oral History of Our Times." He boasted of having accumulated a stack of notebooks that stood 7 feet tall, and he carried brown paper bags with him that, he said, contained research notes.

Joe Gould died in a psychiatric hospital while doing his seagull imitation. Some years later, in a profile article written by Joseph Mitchell for the *New Yorker* magazine, it was revealed that Joe Gould never started his "Oral History," his notebooks were a myth, and his brown bags merely contained other bags and yellowed newspaper clippings. For students with required writing assignments, Joe Gould is a metaphor for the most challenging aspect of any project: how to get started.

First of all, familiarize yourself with Exhibit 1, which shows a flowchart referring to specific chapters and selections in this book that you can refer to as needed. The table of contents (at the beginning of this book) shows the specialized sections and their location in each chapter, and there is a list of exhibits

EXHIBIT 1 Flowchart to walk you through writing papers

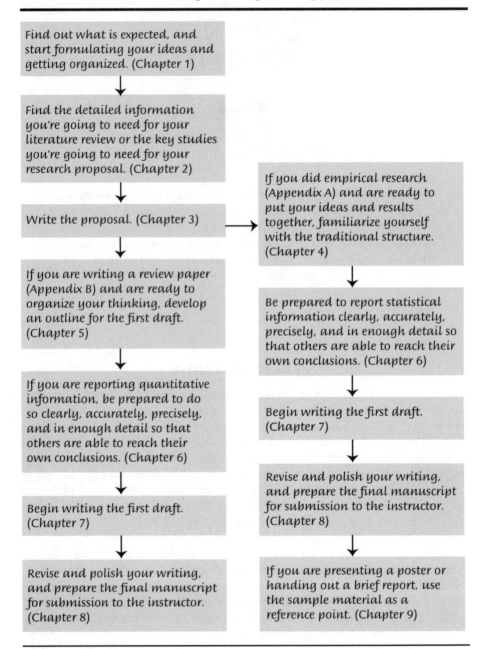

following the table of contents. The index (at the back of the book) lists specific terms should you need to find a particular topic. There are also examples throughout the book. Chapter Three contains sample proposals for a research project and a literature review paper. Appendix A shows a final research report (Jane Doe's), and Appendix B, a final review paper (John Smith's); both of the appendixes are tabbed so that they are easier to find. Chapter Nine shows a poster and a two-page handout describing Jane's research.

To begin your project, you need some clear objectives. Here is a checklist of questions to focus your approach:

- ◆ What is the purpose of the required assignment?
- ◆ Do I choose the theme or topic, or will it be assigned by the instructor?
- ◆ How long should the final paper be?
- ◆ Will interim papers (for example, a proposal and progress reports) be required; how long should they be, and when are they due?
- ◆ When is the final manuscript due, and how does this date mesh with my other assignments (for example, exams and other papers)?

You can talk with other students about their impressions, but the one person who knows *exactly* what is expected of you is the instructor. Before you boot up your computer or sharpen any pencils, meet with the instructor, articulate what you understand the assignment to be, talk about your ideas for a topic, and ask if you are on the right path. One instructor wrote to us that many of his students were reluctant to take this initial step, even though they hadn't a clue about a topic. But those who did come in, even without an idea for a topic, benefited from the meeting and, in most cases, went away with at least the beginning of a direction for their work.

Focusing on Your Objective

Once you have a topic, thinking through the assignment will sharpen your intellectual process. To help you focus on your particular objective, it is well to understand the differences between the research report and the review paper. We suggest you pause at this point and read Jane Doe's research report in Appendix A and John Smith's literature review paper in Appendix B, as we will be referring to them repeatedly. Let us start with the general differences between the research report and the review paper (see Exhibit 2), so you can focus your efforts on whichever project you have been assigned.

One obvious distinction highlighted in Exhibit 2 is that a literature search forms the core of the review paper, whereas empirical data form the core of the research report. Empirical research generally requires a preliminary literature review, but it typically involves retrieving only a few key studies that will serve as theoretical starting points. To give you an idea of how a literature search might be done, Chapter Two begins with an example. The point, however, is that you can expect to spend more time retrieving abstracts

EXHIBIT 2   *Differences between research reports and review papers*

Research Report	*Review Paper*
1. Is based on data that you have collected; literature search involving only a few key studies	1. Is based exclusively on literature search; no hard data of your own to interpret, unless you are counting and summarizing the information
2. Is structured to follow the traditional form described in Chapter Four	2. Is structured by you to fit your particular topic, based on an outline you prepared (described in Chapter Five)
3. Reports your own research findings and conclusions to others in enough detail so they can draw their own conclusions	3. Puts the literature you review into the context of your own insights to bring coherence to the material

and articles online, and probably more time in the library reading and taking notes, if you are writing a review paper. Another reason to spend time in the library is to peruse relevant material such as encyclopedias and other general reference works in the stacks (the shelves throughout the library). If you are writing a senior thesis or a master's thesis, you will be expected to do more than just a cursory search of the literature. We will show how in the next chapter.

A second distinction is that the structure of the research report is expected to conform to a general tradition that has evolved over many years, typically including an abstract, an introduction, a method section, a results section, a discussion of the results, and a list of the references cited. If you open a psychological research journal, you will see examples of this standard structure; Jane's research report is also an example. Review papers are generally more flexible, because it is not always evident, even to experienced writers, how a final manuscript will take shape until they are able to take a thoughtful overall view of the content. Another reason for the flexibility of review papers is that their objectives may be different, so there are several different kinds of literature reviews.

To give a sense of the possible kinds of literature reviews, Duke University psychologist Harris M. Cooper has described the following objectives and categories:[1]

♦ The *focus* of the literature review is the material on which the reviewer wants to concentrate; there may be more than one focal point in the review. Literature reviews in psychology tend to focus on research

---

[1]H. M. Cooper, (1988). Organizing knowledge syntheses: A taxonomy of literature reviews. *Knowledge in Society: The International Journal of Knowledge Transfer, 1,* 104–126.

outcomes, research methods, theories, or practices and applications. The center of attention of John's review paper is theories of intelligence, whereas the heart of Jane's abbreviated review is research outcomes involving tipping practices.

♦ The *goal* is what the reviewer hopes to achieve, which generally is to integrate a body of related work by formulating a general statement, resolving conflicting ideas, or bridging the gap between theories by proposing a common linguistic framework. A second goal is to critically analyze the existing literature, and a third is to identify central issues. John's paper seems to have a flavor of all three general goals, and Jane's is primarily integrative, her objective being to lead into her hypotheses and predictions.

♦ The *perspective* is the point of view influencing the discussion, which for simplicity is called either a neutral representation or the espousal of a position. Both sample papers argue a particular view or set of hypotheses, but the arguments are a distillation of ideas and research results expressed in a scientifically detached tone.

♦ The *coverage* is what primarily distinguishes one literature review from another, because reviewers search the literature and make decisions about the suitability of material based on their own specified criteria. Generally speaking, however, the coverage might be said to be exhaustive, exhaustive with selective citation, representative, or central and pivotal. John's review is representative with selective citations, and Jane's review covers only the key studies related to her goal.

♦ The *organization* of the literature review is how the material cited is arranged—for example, historically, conceptually, or methodologically. John's and Jane's reviews are ostensibly an amalgamation of the conceptual and methodological arrangement. John's paper also attempts to give a flavor of the evolution of ideas in the operationalization of research concepts.

♦ The intended *audience* is the target group to whom the review is addressed, which might be specialized scholars, general scholars, practitioners and policymakers, or the general public. For both John and Jane, the instructor is the audience, who we assume is a scholar with general and specialized knowledge and interests. If Jane later presents her research in a poster at a professional meeting that is open to the public, she will have to be careful not to use technical jargon that is incomprehensible to anyone but a general or specialized scholar in psychology.

The final distinction noted in Exhibit 2 is that the review paper puts issues and ideas into the context of a particular theme or thesis, whereas the main objective of the research report is to describe your empirical investigation to others. The theme in a research report often involves testable hypotheses with explicit predictions, but a report may also be an exploratory study or a purely descriptive investigation (there is more on these distinctions later in this book). If there are hypotheses, then what you found in your research should be put in the context of your predictions.

Scheduling Time

Once you have a clear sense of your objective, the next step is to set some deadlines so you do not end up like Joe Gould, who was so paralyzed by inertia that he accomplished nothing. You know your own energy level and thought patterns, so play to your strengths. Are you a morning person? If so, block out some time to work on your writing early in the day. Do you function better at night? Then use the late hours of quiet to your advantage. Allow extra time for other pursuits by setting realistic dates by which you can reasonably expect to complete each major part of your assignment. Write the dates on your calendar; some students prefer to post the dates over their desks as daily reminders.

In planning your schedule, give yourself ample time to do a good job. Patience will pay off by making you feel more confident as you complete each task and move on to the next one. How do you know what tasks to schedule? Because writing a literature review usually requires spending time online and in the library accumulating material, reading it, and taking notes, you will need to leave ample time for these tasks. Here are some ideas about what to schedule on your calendar if you are writing a review paper and are first required to submit a proposal:

- ◆ Completion of preliminary literature search for proposal
- ◆ Completion of proposal
- ◆ Completion of literature search
- ◆ Completion of library work (full-text articles, encyclopedias, handbooks, etc.)
- ◆ Completion of an outline for first draft
- ◆ Completion of first draft
- ◆ Completion of revised draft(s)
- ◆ Completion of final typed manuscript

If you are writing a research report based on an empirical investigation, you need to set aside time for the ethics review, the implementation of the research, and the data analysis. Here is a list of these and other tasks that must be scheduled if you will be doing empirical research and are first required to submit a proposal:

- ◆ Completion of preliminary literature search for proposal
- ◆ Completion of proposal for research
- ◆ Completion of ethics review
- ◆ Implementation of data collection
- ◆ Completion of data collection

- ◆ Completion of data analysis
- ◆ Completion of an outline for first draft
- ◆ Completion of first draft
- ◆ Completion of revised draft(s)
- ◆ Completion of final typed manuscript (and poster and handouts, if required)

Note that both lists of tasks allow time between the first and final drafts so that you can distance yourself from your writing. Organizing, writing, and revising will take time. Library research does not always go smoothly; a book or a journal article you need might be unavailable. Data collection and analysis can also run into snags. Other problems might be that the ethics review takes longer than you expected, or you are asked to resubmit your proposal, or research subjects do not cooperate, or a computer you need is down, or research material you need is hard to find. These schedules allow you time to cope with unforeseen problems like these and time to return to your writing assignment with a fresh perspective as you polish the first draft and check for errors in logic, flow, spelling, punctuation, and grammar. By scheduling your time in this way, you should not feel pressured by imaginary deadlines—or surprised as the real deadline approaches.

If you get started early, you will also have time to track down hard-to-find material or to locate a test you need. If you want to use a specific test protected by copyright, you will need to give yourself time to get permission from the publisher to use the test. Although tests that require advanced training to administer or interpret are usually unavailable to undergraduates, a great many others are available to students. There are, in fact, general reference books that contain sample measures, and you can ask a reference librarian for suggestions on how to identify and locate these books in the library.

For a comprehensive catalog of available tests and measures that you can find in journal articles and reports, you might look at the six-volume *Directory of Unpublished Experimental Mental Measures,* published by the American Psychological Association from 1995 to 1996. The "unpublished" in the title means that the instrument is generally available without a fee or special credentials. For example, Volume 6, compiled by B. A. Goldman and D. F. Mitchell, lists nearly 1,700 psychological instruments that are available for use in a wide variety of research situations, including measures of educational, psychological, social, and vocational adjustment and measures of aptitude, attitude, concept meaning, creativity, personality, problem solving, status, and so on. Exhibit 3 shows the records of six measures from this volume, and enough information is given to help you track down any particular instrument.

Starting early may also give you time to tackle data analysis procedures that are not in the course textbook. There will also be time to e-mail a researcher and request any follow-up articles that are still unpublished, if you think you need them. Many students are surprised to learn that they can actually communicate

EXHIBIT 3   *Synopses of experimental mental measures*

3678
Test Name: JOB CAREER KEY
Purpose: To provide a test of information about a wide variety of occupations.
Number of Items: 157
Format: A multiple-choice format is used
Reliability: Kuder-Richardson formulas ranged from .43 to .91. Test–retest (4 months) reliability ($N = 19$) was .62.
Author: Yanico, B. J., and Hardin, S. I.
Article: College students' self-estimated and actual knowledge of gender traditional and nontraditional occupation: A replication and extension.
Journal: *Journal of Vocational Behavior*, June 1986, *28*(3), 229–240.
Related Research: Blank, J. R. (1978). Job-career key: A test of occupational information. *Vocational Guidance Quarterly, 27,* 6–17.

3723
Test Name: MEIER BURNOUT ASSESSMENT
Purpose: To measure college student burnout.
Number of Items: 27
Format Employs a true-false format.
Reliability: Cronbach's alpha was .83.
Validity: Correlations with other variables ranged from -.13 to .62 ($N = 360$).
Author: McCarthy, M. E., et al.
Article: Psychological sense of community and student burnout.
Journal: *Journal of College Student Development*, May 1990, *31*(3), 211–216
Related Research: Meier, S. T., & Schmeck, R. R. (1985). The burned-out college student: A descriptive profile. *Journal of College Student Personnel, 25,* 63–69.

3705
Test Name: COMPUTER ANXIETY SCALE
Purpose: To measure the perception held by students of their anxiety in different situations related to computers.
Number of Items: 20
Format: Each item is rated on a 5-point scale ranging from *not at all* to *very much*. All items are presented.
Reliability: Test-retest (10 weeks) reliability was .77. Coefficient alpha was .97.
Author: Marcoulides, G. A.
Article: Measuring computer anxiety: The Computer Anxiety Scale.
Journal: *Educational and Psychological Measurement,* Autumn 1989, *49*(3), 733–739.
Related Research: Endler, N., & Hunt, J. (1966). Sources of behavioral variance as measured by the S-R Inventory of Anxiousness. *Psychological Bulletin, 65,* 336–339.

3993
Test Name: DATING ANXIETY SURVEY
Purpose: To assess dating anxiety in males and females.
Number of Items: 23
Format: Responses are made on a 7-point Likert scale, 1 (*being least anxious*) to 7 (*being extreme anxiety*). Includes three subscales: passive, active, and dating.
Reliability: Coefficient alphas ranged from .87 to .93 (males) and from .90 to .92 (females).
Validity: Correlations with other variables ranged from −.38 to .65.
Author: Calvert, J. D., et al.
Article: Psychometric evaluations of the Dating Anxiety Survey: A self-report questionnaire for the assessment of dating anxiety in males and females.
Journal: *Journal of Psychopathology and Behavioral Assessment,* September 1987, *9*(3), 341–350.

3710
Test Name: HASSLES SCALE
Purpose: To identify the personal severity of daily hassles as an index of student stress.
Number of items: 117
Format: Respondents indicate on a 3-point scale the severity of each relevant daily hassle. Provides two scores: frequency and intensity.
Reliability: Average test-retest reliabilities were .79 (frequency) and .48 (intensity).
Author: Elliott, T. R., and Gramling, S. E.
Article: Personal assertiveness and the effects of social support among college students.
Journal: *Journal of Counseling Psychology,* October 1990, *37*(4), 427–436.
Related Research: Kanner, A., et al. (1981). Comparison of two modes of stress measurement: Daily hassles and uplifts versus major life events. *Journal of Behavioral Medicine, 4,* 1–39.

4431
Test Name: PROCRASTINATION INVENTORY
Purpose: To measure procrastination in work-study, household chores, and interpersonal responsibilities.
Number of Items: 54
Format: Five-point self-rating scales. Sample items presented.
Reliability: Alpha was .91.
Validity: Correlations with other variables ranged from .41 (self-control) to .62 (effective study time).
Author: Stoham-Salomon, V., et al.
Article: You're changed if you do and changed if you don't: Mechanisms underlying paradoxical interventions.
Journal: *Journal of Consulting and Clinical Psychology*, October 1989, *57*(5), 590–598.
Related Research: Sroloff, B. (1963). *An empirical research of procrastination as a state/trait phenomenon.* Unpublished Master's Thesis, Tel-Aviv University, Israel.

Source: From *Directory of Unpublished Experimental Mental Measures, Vol. 6,* by B. A. Goldman and D. F. Mitchell. Copyright © 1995 by the American Psychological Association. Reprinted with permission.

with busy researchers and request the authors' most recent work. If you make a request by e-mail, here are some dos and don'ts:

- Don't ask for something readily available in most college libraries, because it is going to sound as if you were too lazy to look for it.
- Do indicate the nature of your e-mail message (for example, "reprint request"), or it may be deleted as spam without ever being opened.
- Don't write an overly detailed message; say who you are and what you are "requesting" (the polite way of asking), and thank the person in advance.
- Don't expect a lengthy response.
- If you are requesting a reprint, it is likely to be transmitted as a PDF or Word file, so do make sure that your computer can open both of these kinds of files.
- If you receive a response, do thank the person.

Another word of advice: Instructors have heard all the excuses for a late or badly done final term paper, so don't expect much sympathy if you miss the final deadline. If you expect to ask the instructor for a letter of recommendation for graduate school or a job, you certainly do not want to create an impression of yourself as unreliable.

Choosing a Topic

The next step is to come up with a research idea or choose a suitable topic for a literature review. The selection of a research idea or review topic is an integral part of learning, because usually you are free to explore experiences, observations, and ideas to help you focus on specific questions or issues that will sustain your curiosity and interest as you work on your project. There are lots of ways of getting ideas. For example, John notes in his proposal (in Chapter Three) that he first became interested in interpersonal acumen after the instructor's lecture on intelligence, in which she mentioned that she had done empirical research on this topic. Jane mentions a similar situation and also notes her personal interest in tipping behavior (because she has worked as a waitress during summer vacations).

If you are a psychology major or minor, you probably already have lots of questions and ideas regarding why people behave, perceive, or think as they do. But if you are looking around for an idea, and your psychology department invites guest researchers to present colloquia that are open to undergraduate students (they usually are), bring a pencil and paper to jot down any ideas you get. It is also an opportunity to ask the speaker a question, listen to others' questions and the speaker's responses, and if there is an open reception afterward, chat with the speaker. Another way to stimulate your creative mind is to peruse the journals in some specialty area that is of interest to you, and to look in the texts you were required to read in the courses you liked a lot. Approaching this material with an open, inquisitive mind is likely to stimulate creative thinking. However, if you cannot come up with an idea, discuss your dilemma with the instructor and ask for advice.

In considering a suitable topic, beware of a few pitfalls. The following are dos and don'ts that might make your life easier as you start choosing a topic:

◆ Do choose a topic that piques your curiosity.
◆ Do make sure your topic can be covered in the available time and in the assigned number of pages.
◆ Don't choose a topic that you know other students have chosen; you will be competing with them for access to the library's source material.
◆ If you are not already knowledgeable on a topic, do read about it *first* before you try to narrow it for your project.

Narrowing the Topic

Choosing too broad or too narrow a topic for either a literature review or a research project will add difficulties and anxiety and will mean an unsatisfactory result. A proposed review that is too broad—for example, "Sigmund Freud's Life and Times"—would try to cover too much material within the limited framework of the assignment and the time available to complete it. A specific aspect of Freud's theoretical work (assuming you are interested in psychoanalytic writings) would prove a more appropriately narrowed focus for treatment in a review paper for a course on personality theories, abnormal behavior, or psychopathology.

In narrowing the literature review topic, do not limit your discussion to facts that are already well known. Ask yourself what is special about how you plan to approach the assignment. For example, John's review paper is not just a listing of other people's conclusions, but an effort to incorporate his own perspective. It will make the paper stand out when the instructor grades it. There are two further guidelines in narrowing your topic:

◆ Be sure that your topic is not so narrow that reference materials will be hard to find.
◆ Be guided by your instructor's advice because the instructor can help you avoid taking on an unwieldy topic.

If you approach instructors with several concrete ideas, you will usually find them glad to help tailor those ideas so that you, the topic, and the project format are compatible. Here are examples of how you might shape the working title of a term paper on Sigmund Freud:

Unlimited Topic (Much Too Broad)
Freud's Theories of Personality and Abnormal Behavior

Limited to 20-Page Paper
Freud's Theory of Oedipal Conflict Applied to Mental Health

Limited to 10-Page Paper
Freud's Theory of Infantile Sexuality

You can always polish the title later, once you have finished your literature search, have read what you found, and have a better sense of the topic. Here is another example of shaping a topic for a one-semester research course. These are not tentative titles for a proposal, but questions to focus the research:

Unlimited Topic (Too Broad for a Term Project)
How are nonverbal stimuli deciphered?

Slightly Limited Topic
How are certain kinds of nonverbal stimuli deciphered by male and female subjects?

Adequately Limited Topic
How do male and female intro psych students at Podunk U. differ in their ability to decipher photographed facial expressions of joy, disappointment, anger, and fear in a sample of male and female actors?

If you are currently enrolled in a research methods course, your text probably discusses criteria for assessing the merits of hypotheses. A detailed discussion is beyond the scope of this book, but we can mention three criteria:

- ◆ Hypotheses for empirical research should be grounded in credible ideas and facts. In other words, you must do a preliminary literature search to find out whether your ideas are consistent with accepted findings in the scientific literature. If they are not, then you will need to think about the inconsistencies and decide (with the help of the instructor) whether you really have a fresh insight or will need to develop some other hypothesis.
- ◆ State your hypothesis in a precise and focused way. To ensure that you are using technical terms correctly, you can consult resources in the library (encyclopedias of psychology, for example). To ensure that your hypothesis is focused, you can consult your instructor, who will show you how to cut away unwieldy words and ideas.
- ◆ Hypotheses and predictions must be falsifiable if they are incorrect. Those that are not refutable by any conceivable empirical means are considered unscientific. For example, the statement "All behavior is a product of the good and evil lying within us" does not qualify as a valid scientific hypothesis: It is so vague and amorphous that it cannot be subjected to empirical refutation.

Knowing Your Audience and Topic

All professional writers know that they are writing for a particular audience. This knowledge helps them determine the tone and style of their work. Think of a journalist's report of a house fire and contrast it with a short story describing the same event. Knowing one's audience is no less important when the writer is a college student and the project is a literature review or a research report. The audience is your instructor, who is not just any reader, but someone knowledgeable in the area. Thus, you are writing to demonstrate your own acquired knowledge, and also to give evidence of your insights to this sophisticated reader.

If you have questions about the instructor's grading criteria, find out what they are before you start to work. For example, in a course on research methods, one instructor's syllabus listed the following grading criteria for different parts of the finished report (the numbers in parentheses are percentages):

Abstract
  Informativeness (5)
Introduction
  Clarity of purpose (10)
  Literature review (10)
Method
  Adequacy of design (10)
  Quality and completeness of description (10)
Results
  Appropriateness and correctness of analysis (10)
  Use of tables or figures (5)
  Clarity of presentation (10)
Discussion
  Interpretation of results (10)
  Critique/future directions (10)
Miscellaneous
  Organization, style, references, etc. (5)
  Appendix for raw data and calculations (5)

This kind of information enabled the students to concentrate on different parts of the assignment in the same way that the instructor would concentrate on them when evaluating the reports. This information can also serve as a checklist for you to make sure that everything of importance is covered adequately in your finished report. Not every instructor will provide such detailed information about grading, but this manual can help you compose your own checklist based on other information the instructor has provided.

Cultivating an Understanding

Let us assume that you know what your main audience—your instructor—expects of you. Now you must try to develop more than a superficial understanding of your topic. The more you read about it and discuss your ideas with friends, the more you will begin to cultivate an intuitive understanding of the topic. In the next chapter, we describe how to use computerized and library resources to nurture this understanding. Here are two tips to get you started:

- ◆ Some writers find it helpful to keep several index cards handy, or to use sticky notes, for jotting down relevant ideas that suddenly occur to them. This is a good way to keep your topic squarely in your mind.
- ◆ You must also comprehend your source material, so equip yourself with a good desk dictionary, and turn to it routinely whenever you come across an unfamiliar word. It is a habit that will serve you well.

The most comprehensive dictionaries are labeled *unabridged* (which means that they have not been shortened in size by the omission of terms or definitions). The most famous (and most comprehensive) of all unabridged dictionaries in the English language is the multivolume *Oxford English Dictionary* (called for short the *OED*). The hardbound print version is expensive, but you can probably find it in your college library. Some libraries provide electronic access to the *OED*. If you are that rare student who loves obscure origins of words, the *OED* is the place to look.

2

FINDING AND USING REFERENCE MATERIALS

*The literature search is an indispensable step in preparing a
review paper; it is also an essential aspect of a research proposal
as it puts your own ideas in context, building on the existing
work of others. Knowing about the many online and print
resources available will allow you to gauge the effort it will take
to find the information you need. If you know how to retrieve this
information electronically, you can save time and effort.*

Defining the Problem

Let us assume you have an idea for a research project or a review paper, have
spoken about it in a preliminary way with your instructor, and know that you
must produce a written proposal. In the next chapter, we illustrate the nature
of the proposal. Before you begin drafting it, however, you will need to identify and read relevant work on the topic that interests you. To help you, we
begin by looking over the shoulder of a student, named Maya, who is interested in gathering a few key studies to help her formulate one or two hypotheses and write a proposal for a research project. First, we describe how Maya
goes step by step through the process of doing a literature search. Afterward,
we will examine in more detail the resources she used and others that may be
available in college libraries or electronically through library Web sites.

Maya thinks she wants to study a spin-off from the instructor's lecture on
what he called the "Pygmalion experiment," a classic research study by Robert
Rosenthal and Lenore Jacobson. In a book the instructor mentioned, called
Pygmalion in the Classroom, Rosenthal and Jacobson described how, in the
1960s, they had given a standard nonverbal intelligence test to all the children in
a public elementary school in South San Francisco. The teachers were told only
that the test was one of intellectual "blooming," and approximately 20% of the
children (whose names the investigators had picked at random) were represented

to the teachers as showing capability of marked intellectual growth in their performance on this test. In other words, the difference between the supposed potential bloomers and the other students existed solely in the minds of their teachers. The children's performance on the intelligence test was measured after one semester, again after a full academic year, and again after two academic years. The results revealed that, although the greatest differential gain in total intelligence appeared after one school year, the bloomers held an advantage over the other children even after two years. Maya's instructor described these results as an example of what psychologists generally refer to as *expectancy effects*.

Maya mentions her interest in the Pygmalion experiment to the instructor, who suggests she read Rosenthal and Jacobson's book and look up a journal article by Stephen Raudenbush. The instructor is not certain when or where the Raudenbush article was published but thinks it was in the 1980s in the *Journal of Educational Psychology*. He tells Maya that the Raudenbush article is a report of the results of a quantitative literature review (a meta-analysis) of all the Pygmalion experiments up to that time. The instructor advises Maya to use PsycINFO to do an author search to find this article. He also suggests that she look up the terms *expectancy effect* and *Pygmalion experiment* in recent encyclopedias of psychology that the library has, and use PsycINFO again to do a more extensive retrieval of abstracts after she has identified the *limited vocabulary* (also called the *control vocabulary*) that is appropriate to each electronic database. Using the appropriate vocabulary can prevent the frustration of searching with the "wrong" terms, but Maya decides to plunge forward on her own using the terms mentioned by her instructor.

Looking Over Maya's Shoulder

Maya begins by finding her college library's Web page (which typically has a link on the university or college home page) and then finds the online catalog to search for the Rosenthal and Jacobson book. She types "Pygmalion in the classroom" in the search field, indicates that it is a "title," and hits "go." The resulting information gives her the book's call number, which tells her where to find this book in the library's stacks. Whether the book is currently in the library, checked out, or overdue is also indicated. For example, if *Pygmalion in the Classroom* had been checked out by someone a while ago and still not returned, Maya could ask the library to "recall" the book by asking the current user to return it. Fortunately, this book is in the library, and Maya finds it and takes it to the circulation desk to check it out. While there, she asks about the location of encyclopedias of psychology, and the librarian points her to the location of several. She looks up *expectancy effects* in the indexes, reads the material, and finds that expectancy effects are also referred to as *experimenter expectancy effects*, and sometimes as *Rosenthal effects*, since Robert Rosenthal did landmark research on the topic. Maya takes notes, including jotting down relevant references and recommended readings that are cited in the encyclopedia articles, which she will look into later.

EXHIBIT 4 *PsycINFO record of journal article*

Record 1 of 1 in PsycINFO 1984-1987

AN: 1984-16218-001

DT: Journal-Article

TI: Magnitude of teacher expectancy effects on pupil IQ as a function of the credibility of expectancy induction: A synthesis of findings from 18 experiments.

AU: **Raudenbush,-Stephen-W**

SO: Journal-of-Educational-Psychology. 1984 Feb; Vol 76(1): 85-97

PB: US: American Psychological Assn.

IS: 0022-0663

PY: 1984

AB: Meta-analysis was used to examine the variability in the outcomes of experiments testing the effects of teacher expectancy on pupil IQ. The tenuous process of expectancy induction, wherein researchers supply teachers with information designed to elevate their expectancies for children actually selected at random, is viewed as problematic in "Pygmalion" experiments, as developed by R. Rosenthal and L. Jacobson (1968). It was hypothesized that the better teachers know their pupils at the time of expectancy induction, the smaller the treatment effect would be. Data strongly support this hypothesis. Hypotheses that the type of IQ test (groups vs. individual) and type of test administrator (aware vs blind to expectancy-inducing information) influence experimental results were not supported. The hypothesis that expectancy effects are larger for children in Grades 1 and 2 than for children in Grades 3-6 was supported. However, significant effects reappeared at Grade 7. Theoretical implications and questions for future meta-analytic research are discussed. (57 ref) (PsycINFO Database Record (c) 2000 APA, all rights reserved)(unassigned)

To find the article by Stephen Raudenbush, Maya again uses her computer to access the library's reference databases. On the main page of the library's Web site, she finds PsycINFO listed under "electronic databases" (or, in some libraries, "e-resources"). Many libraries list alphabetically all the databases they subscribe to, so you can scroll down to the one you are looking for. If the databases are organized by academic field (such as anthropology, marketing, psychology, etc.), then PsycINFO usually comes up first under psychology. Maya clicks on PsycINFO and checks the place that says "Author"; she types in "Raudenbush" and clicks on the SEARCHES button. The result is a long list of published works by this author, each item on the list linking to a PsycINFO record that also provides an abstract of the work. Maya scrolls down the list until she recognizes the article that her instructor mentioned and prints out the PsycINFO record (shown in Exhibit 4). The complete version of this particular article is unavailable on PsycINFO's companion resource database, called PsycARTICLES, but she will look it up later in the college library and photocopy the relevant parts. Given the information in the PsycINFO record of the article (journal name, year, volume, and page numbers), she knows how to track it down in the library.

Having done all this, Maya has mastered about all the skills she will need to use any other electronic database to do a detailed search. For now, she begins her search of the literature in the PsycINFO database. The PsycINFO screen may vary from library to library, depending on the type of subscription the library has to this service. Maya begins not by searching right away, but by using the THESAURUS SEARCH button on PsycINFO to tell her what search terms to use. She types in "expectancy effects" (putting quotes around the pair of words to indicate that she wants the search engine to look for the combination, not just for the single word *expectancy* and the single word *effects*) and presses ENTER. (Most search engines require either quotes, which Maya used, or a search command.) However, Maya's exact term is not found (it is not part of the control vocabulary), and the closest terms listed are not relevant to her search. Next, she types in "teacher expectancy." This is another "wrong" term, so it is not found. However, she finds that "teacher expectations" is a related term, so she clicks on it. A few more choices are listed; she clicks on "expectations" to find the terms that will be most useful to her when searching this topic in PsycINFO.

Maya decides to start with "experimenter expectations," so she puts a check in the box beside this term and clicks on SEARCH. The program automatically searches on this term, and it returns 158 items. By default, the most recent articles are first. Maya runs the search again, using the same term but this time limiting the search to "journal articles only." The list is pared down to 125, still a lot of records, too many for one page: The results pages typically return only a portion of the complete list of citations per page, and Maya's screen shows 25 citations per page. She decides to look at all 125 because she has to scroll down only 5 pages to do so. She puts a check in the box before each citation that looks promising for her working hypothesis, 7 citations in all, and she presses the VIEW MARKED RECORDS button for each of them. With this list, she selects from a drop-down menu the "citation and abstract" (an abstract is a paragraph or two summarizing the article). She reads the abstracts, selects 5 articles as relevant, and clicks on SAVE/PRINT/EMAIL records. If she were at a library computer, she could either print out the list of citations and abstracts or e-mail the results to herself. However, because she is at her own computer, she saves the file to her drive. She sees that she will have to indicate the citation and abstract *again* before she can e-mail, print, or save the information; otherwise, she will save only the citation.

Using the Online Catalog and Browsing the Stacks

Maya began by using the library's online catalog to find *Pygmalion in the Classroom* and then went to the stacks for this and other relevant books. Libraries in the United States do not all use the same online program for their

EXHIBIT 5   Library of Congress online record of book

```
LC Control Number:      68019667
Type of Material:       Book (Print, Microform, Electronic, etc.)
Personal Name:          Rosenthal, Robert, 1933-
Main Title:             Pygmalion in the classroom; teacher expectation
                        and pupils' intellectual development [by] Robert
                        Rosenthal [and] Lenore Jacobson.
Published/Created:      New York, Holt, Rinehart and Winston [1968]
Related Names:          Jacobson, Lenore, joint author.
Description:            xi, 240 p. illus. 23 cm.
ISBN:                   0030688051
                        0030686857 (college ed.)
Notes:                  Bibliography: p. 219-229.
Subjects:               Prediction of scholastic success.
                        Children--Intelligence levels.
LC Classification:      LB1131 .R585
Dewey Class No.:        372.12/64 19
                        ----------------------
CALL NUMBER:            LB1131 .R585
                        Copy 1
-- Request in:          Jefferson or Adams Bldg General or Area Studies
                        Reading Rms
-- Status:              Not Charged
```

---

automated card catalogs, but they usually provide the same basic information to patrons. If you go to the Web site of the Library of Congress Online Catalog in Washington, DC (www.lcWeb.loc.gov/catalog), and look up the Rosenthal and Jacobson book, you will find the detailed record shown in Exhibit 5. Before the existence of online catalogs, all libraries had card catalogs (usually near the reference desk) consisting of miles and miles of index cards. The information shown in Exhibit 5 may be more extensive than what you see in your library's online record. The most significant information for most students is the call number, near the bottom of this particular online record: LB1131.R585. This code means that, to find this book, you would go to the LB section of the stacks and, next, to the specific section in numerical (1131) and then alphanumerical order (R585).

If you are interested, the "LC Control Number" is an internal Library of Congress code. The "Type of Material" indicates that this is a book available in several formats. "Personal Name" shows the name and year of birth of the first author. The title and subtitle of the book are next shown, followed by the list of authors in the order in which they appear on the title page. Then follows the location and name of the publisher (New York, Holt, Rinehart and Winston) and the date of copyright (1968). "Description" indicates the number of prefatory pages (xi) and the length of the book (240 pages), and that it contains figures or other illustrations (illus.) and stands 23 cm high on the shelf. The "ISBN" (for International Standard Book Number) refers to the code numbers assigned by the publisher that identify the book. The "Dewey Class No." is another way of cataloging the book (more about this later), but it was the "LC Classification" (Library of Congress call number) that Maya's library used to catalog this book. Other useful information gives buildings or places where copies of this book can be found and a note that the book is currently available ("Not Charged").

Maya went to the stacks to find this book and asked a librarian where the encyclopedias of psychology were shelved. It is useful to know where photocopiers are located and whether you need to bring coins or purchase a card in order to use them. It is a lot easier to photocopy a page from a journal or book than to copy lengthy passages by hand, and having a photocopy will ensure that you have the information as it appears in the original source. If you don't know how to access the library's electronic databases from your own computer, you can ask about this and the user name and password that are typically required. If there is a *reference desk*, it is where you go to find staff members who are true generalists and able to answer all manner of questions or at least point you to sources to help you answer them yourself. They may suggest works that are "not circulated" but can be used in a specified section of the library. Suppose you wanted to find information about a psychological test; they might point you to the *Mental Measurements Yearbook* for such information as the population for intended use, forms, cost, author, publisher, cross-references to previous editions, and references to authoritative reviews, journal articles, books, and dissertations that discuss the test. If you want a book or journal that is unavailable, you can also ask at the reference desk about an interlibrary loan.

The *circulation desk* was where Maya went to check out her book; it is also where you go to return materials and take care of overdue notices. Bring a photo ID with you. There is also the *reserve area*, which is for books, photocopies of articles, and other material that instructors have placed "on hold" or "on reserve" (not to be circulated). You can examine this material only in the reserve area and for a specified period (2 hours, for example). *Current periodicals* is where you will find recent issues of journals, magazines, and newspapers. However, it is also possible to view some articles and other materials electronically, a method that not only conserves space but also prevents the problem of missing or damaged copies. These electronic databases (discussed later in this chapter) expand the storehouse of available information as libraries share their resources through interconnected computers. (For a list of definitions of common terms and jargon used on the Web, see Exhibit 6.) We mentioned interlibrary loan above: Most libraries belong to groups of libraries that share books and other materials and reciprocate services.

The Library of Congress call number that Maya looked up is one of two main systems of classification that are most often used in U.S. libraries. The other is the Dewey decimal system. You need the proper call number because

EXHIBIT 6 *Common terms and jargon on the Web*

---

attachment: a digitally coded file that is downloaded when you specifically open an add-on to an e-mail message; the attachment might contain words, images, or, in a worst case scenario, a hidden virus.

browser: a program that is used to display Web pages.

cache: a place on the computer's hard drive where images and text from visited Web pages are stored to speed up the process of downloading the next time they are visited. Caches can, however, clutter the hard drive, particularly when information on the Web pages is constantly updated, so it is a good idea to clean the cache routinely.

cookies: bits of personalized information left on the hard drive by some Web sites so they can track visitors online (some Web sites will not admit visitors unless they agree to accept a cookie). There are cookie cleanup programs (we use Norton Systemworks) to send this clutter into oblivion.

database: a collection of data, such as the reference databases shown in Exhibit 9.

firewall: a system that protects online computers from outside hackers who want to steal information or create a launching pad for destructive signals to Web sites.

full-text database: textual material that can be electronically perused in its entirety, such as the complete content of a journal article, a book, a dictionary, or an encyclopedia.

html: the coded language (hypertext markup language) used to create Web pages.

http: acronym for *hypertext transfer protocol,* the prefix (http://) of many URLs; it signifies the way that computers communicate with one another on the Internet.

hyperlink: a coded image (an icon or a button) or a coded word or phrase (usually in blue and underlined) that changes to a hand when you move your mouse pointer over it; clicking the hyperlink transports you to another place.

Internet service provider: the company or organization providing access to the Internet, such as AOL (America Online) and MSN (Microsoft Network), or a telephone or cable company.

JPEG: acronym for Joint Photographic Experts Group, which is the most popular format on the Internet for photos because it supports 24-bit color and subtle variations in brightness and hue.

online search: the use of a computer and a search engine to retrieve information.

PDF: acronym for *Portable Document Format,* it retains the look of the original document and is viewed by means of the Acrobat Reader installed on your computer (or available for free from http://www.adobe.com).

search engine: a program that takes key words, queries an internal index, and returns a set of Web documents. A popular search engine is Google (http://www.google.com); if you click on HELP CENTRAL, you will find menus with search help instructions, terminology, and advanced search tips. Other search engines include Yahoo, HotBot, AltaVista, Lycos, InfoSeek, Excite, and Metacrawler.

spam: unsolicited e-mail that is automatically sent to all those on an address list.

URL: acronym for *uniform resource locator,* which is another name for the Web address. The URL of a helpful Web site created at the University of Waterloo, which contains links to national and international psychological societies (including the American Psychological Association and the American Psychological Society, which post information about student funding and career planning), is http://www.lib.uwaterloo.ca/society/psychol_soc.html. If you are interested in the field of social psychology, you might check the Social Psychology Network at http://www. socialpsychology.org, created at Wesleyan University by Dr. Scott Plous.

viruses: damaging codes that invade a computer's hard drive when an infected attachment or a contaminated file is opened. Some viruses, called *worms,* copy themselves and spread rapidly in the hard drive; others, called *Trojan horses,* assume the appearance of normal files but secretly wipe the hard drive clean. As a safeguard against viruses, be cautious about what you download or open, and install (and routinely update, usually weekly) antivirus software to check attachments before you open them and, in a worst case scenario, to find and try to repair damage to your hard drive.

EXHIBIT 7   Two systems of classification used in U.S. libraries

Library of Congress System		Dewey Decimal System	
A	General works	000	General works
B	Philosophy, religion, and psychology	100	Philosophy
C	General history	200	Religion
D	Foreign history	300	Social sciences
E-F	America	400	Language
G	Geography and anthropology	500	Natural sciences
H	Social sciences	600	Technology
J	Political science	700	Fine arts
K	Law	800	Literature
L	Education	900	History and geography
M	Music		
N	Fine arts		
P	Language and literature		
Q	Science		
R	Medicine		
S	Agriculture		
T	Technology		
U	Military science		
V	Naval science		
Z	Bibliography and library science		

the stacks are coded according to Library of Congress or Dewey decimal categories that coincide with call numbers, and the call number is also printed on the bottom of the book's spine. Exhibit 7 shows these two main systems of classification. For psychology students, the systems may be puzzling because psychological material is classified under several different headings. The Library of Congress system divides material into 20 major groups, and abnormal psychology books, for example, can be found under BF or RC. The Dewey decimal system classifies material under 10 headings (and abnormal psychology can be found in the 157 class).

Some libraries protect their collection of books by restricting access to the stacks. If you find yourself unable to access the stacks directly, you submit a form that lists the call number of the book you want to use and a staff member retrieves it for you. If you are allowed to browse in the stacks, refer to Exhibit 8. It shows the cataloging of specific areas by both systems. Browsing can lead you to a valuable but unexpected book or to a pertinent quote that illustrates some idea or point. But do not get sidetracked by irrelevant material; keep focused on the purpose of your search.

EXHIBIT 8 *Cataloging of psychological materials in U.S. libraries*

Library of Congress System		*Dewey Decimal System*	
BF	Abnormal psychology	00-	Artificial intelligence
	Child psychology	13-	Parapsychology
	Cognition	15-	Abnormal psychology
	Comparative psychology		Child psychology
	Environmental psychology		Cognitive psychology
	Motivation		Comparative psychology
	Parapsychology		Environmental psychology
	Perception		Industrial psychology
	Personality		Motivation
	Physiological psychology		Perception
	Psycholinguistics		Personality
	Psychological statistics		Physiological psychology
HF	Industrial psychology	30-	Family
	Personnel management		Psychology of women
HM	Social psychology		Social psychology
HQ	Family	37-	Educational psychology
	Psychology of women		Special education
LB	Educational psychology	40-	Psycholinguistics
LC	Special education	51-	Statistics
Q	Artificial intelligence	61-	Psychiatry
	Physiological psychology		Psychotherapy
QA	Mathematical statistics	65-	Personnel management
RC	Abnormal psychology		
	Psychiatry		
	Psychotherapy		
T	Personnel management		

PsycINFO, PsycARTICLES, PsycBOOKS, and PsycEXTRA

Maya used PsycINFO, the American Psychological Association's primary abstract database. The advantage of electronic databases like this one, as she discovered, is that you can search to your heart's content. Even if you do not have your own computer, the library usually has a bank of computers reserved for students. Because you may have to wait your turn to use one, you might ask whether there are computers in other locations that you can use to communicate with the automated system. If you have your own computer, you need to find out how to access these resources from your room. PsycINFO and other electronic databases each have their own limited vocabulary, which is appropriate to the particular database. For example, the print version of PsycINFO's limited vocabulary is the *Thesaurus of Psychological Index Terms* (published by the American Psychological Association, or APA), which is typically available in libraries that subscribe to PsycINFO. Libraries that use the Library of Congress system usually have a copy of the *Library of Congress Subject Heading Index,* which lists the limited vocabulary used in the card catalogs.

There are also full-text databases, but few that are free online. The records in PsycINFO typically have a "journal link" that takes the user to the journal home page on the publisher's site, where you find out if the full text is free or not. (Some publishers put their journals up for free after an embargo period.) Maya can count on getting free full-text articles from journals to which her library has purchased access and to full-text journals available on InfoTrac College Edition (packaged with this edition of *Writing Papers*). We will have more to say about InfoTrac College Edition in the next section, but PsycARTICLES is the APA's full-text database for journals that, as of 2004, went back to 1986. The APA is currently expanding this database, with the hope of going back to Volume 1, Issue 1, by December 2005. The APA also offers universities the opportunity to subscribe to another database called PsycBOOKS, which lists books and a full-text record (PDF) for each chapter in the book for nearly all books published by the APA, some historic books in the public domain, and 1,500 entries in the APA's *Encyclopedia of Psychology.* Another new APA database is called PsycEXTRA and provides records and some full-text access to the "gray literature" (work that is unpublished or hard to find) that is not covered in PsycINFO and is outside the peer-review literature (conference papers, newspapers, technical reports, government reports, etc.).

Exhibit 9 gives a flavor of some of the many electronic databases that may be available to students through their library's Web page. There are databases for just about every discipline and area of interest, and it is easy and fun to use them. Here are some tips:

- ◆ Begin by writing down your questions, and then make a list of words or phrases you want to try as search terms.
- ◆ Scan the list of the databases that are available to you online; print the list if you can, to avoid having to remember them or endlessly going back and forth.
- ◆ Put a check mark next to any other databases that look relevant now or that might be of interest later on.
- ◆ As you search, keep a record so that you don't backtrack without realizing it; list the abstract or index, the years searched, and the search terms that you used.

EXHIBIT 9 *Reference databases available electronically*

Name	*Coverage*
Academic Search Premier	Full-text data of many scholarly publications in social science, the humanities, education, computer science, engineering, language and linguistics, arts and literature, medical science, and ethnic studies.
AskERIC	Bibliographic records of research reports, conference papers, teaching guides, books, and journal articles in education from preschool to the doctoral level; ERIC is an acronym for Educational Resources Information Center.
booksinprint.com	Full-text reviews of books in print, as well as out-of-print listings over the last decade.
britannica.com	Full-text database for *Encyclopedia Britannica* and *Merriam-Webster's Collegiate Dictionary.*
Census Lookup	Produced by the U.S. Census Bureau, offers access to data tables for specific types of geographic areas from the most recent Census of Population and Housing.
CQ Library	Full-text database for *CQ Weekly* and *CQ Researcher,* which provide legislative news about what is happening on Capitol Hill.
EDGAR	Acronym for Electronic Data Gathering, Analysis, and Retrieval System, this is the Securities and Exchange Commission's database of electronic filings.
Electronic Human Relations Area Files	Acronym is eHRAF; this nonprofit institution at Yale University is a consortium of educational, research, cultural, and government agencies in over 30 countries that provides ethnographic and related information by culture and subject.
GPO Access	U.S. Government Printing Office full-text documents and other informational links.
Harrison's Online	Full text of *Harrison's Principles of Internal Medicine,* a well-known medical textbook.
InfoTrac College Edition	Full-text database, packaged with *Writing Papers in Psychology* (seventh edition), provides free four-month access to the *Annual Review of Psychology* and many journals listed by discipline.
Internet Grateful Med	Health-related search information, including links to MEDLINE (national and international references to millions of articles in medicine, biomedicine, and related fields), AIDSLINE, HISTLINE (history of medicine online), and other Web sites.

◆ If you can, copy what you find on a disk that you can scan again later; before you open this file (or download it to your own hard drive), use your antivirus program to ensure that the file is not infected.

◆ Do not just make a citation list of relevant work; also read what you are going to cite because the instructor will wonder whether you have read it.

EXHIBIT 9   *Continued*

Name	Coverage
JSTOR	Full text of periodicals in ecology, economics, education, finance, history, mathematics, political science, and population studies.
LEXIS-NEXIS Academic UNIVerse	Full text of news reports, including business, medical, political, financial, and legal; a convenient source of news reports by topic areas.
MathSciNet	Research literature in mathematics, with an emphasis on data in *Mathematical Reviews* and *Current Mathematical Publications.*
NCJRS Database	National Criminal Justice Reference Service database, including summaries of publications on criminal justice.
New Grove Dictionary	Full text of *The New Grove Dictionary of Music and Musicians* and *The New Grove Dictionary of Opera.*
OED Online	Full text of 20-volume *Oxford English Dictionary* and additions.
ProQuest Direct	Records of scholarly journals, periodicals, newspapers, and magazines in the University of Michigan archives, including charts, maps, photos, and some literature in full-text format.
PsycARTICLES	The American Psychological Association's full-text database of APA journal articles.
PsycBOOKS	The American Psychological Association's full-text database of chapters in books published by the APA, some historic books in the public domain, and the 1,500 entries in the APA's *Encyclopedia of Psychology.*
PsycEXTRA	The American Psychological Association's database of the "gray literature," including many full-text records (conference papers, newspapers, technical reports, government reports, etc.).
PsycINFO	The American Psychological Association's abstract database, including every abstract created by the APA back to 1887 in all areas of psychology.
ScienceDirect	Fee-based database of Elsevier journals and many more.
Web of Science	Access to *Social Sciences Citation Index (SSCI),* the parent source of titles of works and names of authors, from 1989 to the present, as well as the *Science Citation Index* (also from 1989 forward).

InfoTrac College Edition and the Web of Science

We mentioned another useful electronic database, InfoTrac College Edition, which is packaged with the seventh edition of *Writing Papers in Psychology* (http://www.infotrac-college.com). To register on the log-in screen, you enter a user name that you select and the password that came with your book (write down the user name and password for later use). After registering, you will find yourself at the keyboard search screen, where you type in search terms. You also specify the search strategy form you want InfoTrac College Edition to use; for example, indicating "in entire article content" will do a more extensive search for you than just indicating "in title, citation abstract." The browser also keeps a record of your searches under "History," so you can highlight one of your previous searches and press VIEW to see the results of that particular search. Previous searches can be useful if you want to try a different variation of a search. Another option is to put a check mark in the box beside "to refereed publications," which means that only articles that have been reviewed by journal consultants (called *referees*) will be listed.

Once you have the list of refereed journal articles, you can set aside the titles you want to review by clicking in the box in front of each promising item. Then, using VIEW MARK LIST from the menu at the top, you can retrieve this marked subset. The retrieval options are under the marked list, at the bottom of the page. If you click the FULL ARTICLE option and also e-mail the article to yourself, you will receive a plain-text version of each available article, one e-mail per article. There is also the option to print the marked articles in plain-text format, although you may prefer to save paper (and printing costs) by reading them first on-screen on your computer. Next to the citations in your marked list, two icons (tiny pictures) may appear. One indicates that there is a plain text of the article available (this is usually the case); the other looks like a little camera, indicating there are graphics included in the plain text. The graphics are shown in a reduced size in the text, but you can click on them to view their full size.

There are other tools available on InfoTrac College Edition if you click on the link to an article. At the end of the plain-text version that comes up, you can often use the Acrobat Reader (a special computer program) to see a PDF replica of the original article as it appeared in the journal. Most browsers have the Acrobat Reader already installed, but you can download it for free at www.adobe.com. The PDF format is very convenient, but it can be time-consuming to download. If you download articles in this format, save them to your drive or disc, because they are easier to read than the plain-text version that is e-mailed or appears with the link from the marked list. At the end of each article is a menu of still more articles that are linked to related topics, which vary with each article. You may not need these articles now, but they may be useful for researching and writing your paper later.

If you needed to do a more comprehensive search for a meta-analysis or a dissertation, another useful reference database in Exhibit 9 is the Web of Science, which provides access to relatively recent records in the *Social Sciences Citation Index (SSCI)*, *Science Citation Index (SCI)*, and *Arts & Humanities Citation Index (A&HCI)*. These databases are useful if you want to track down studies that followed up on an older study that you have read about in your textbook. Once you are into the Web of Science, you can click on the TUTORIAL button to get guidance, or click on the FULL SEARCH (a general search) or the EASY

SEARCH button (a more limited search of articles on a specific topic, person, or address). This kind of search is called an *ancestry search* because you are tracking down "ancestral" citations of an older article or a book. For example, if you looked up *Pygmalion in the Classroom,* you would get a long list of citations of this book. Many libraries also contain the print version of *SSCI*, which is quite easy to use. Code letters are used to indicate the nature of the citation, such as *D* for "discussion" (conference item), *L* for "letter," *M* for "meeting abstract," *N* for "technical note," *RP* for "reprint," and *W* for "computer review." Where there is no code letter indicated, this means the citation is an article, a report, a technical paper, or the like.

Once you are familiar with PsycINFO or InfoTrac College Edition, you should find it relatively easy to use other electronic databases to search for information. Here are some more tips:

- ◆ Don't start out by using Google or Yahoo for your search and then rely on any documents that appear. Search engines like these seek what are called *statistic Web pages,* or thin, digitized layers of information that do not have search functions of their own. The electronic databases in Exhibit 9 are part of what is called the *deep Web,* which means they surface only when you make database queries from within the sites. Google, Yahoo, and similar search engines are not equipped to go beneath the surface; the material you turn up will not be what your instructor expects for a literature review.
- ◆ Typically, there are also edifying Web sites linked to textbooks, which are designed to help you make optimal use of a textbook and other course material. When you are using these Web sites, remember that you have a particular objective, so don't get distracted by tantalizing games (play with them after the semester is over).
- ◆ If you are in a department that has many active researchers on the faculty, it is possible that one of them is working on the very problem that interests you. To find out, ask your instructor, and also ask if it will be OK to approach that person. If the answer is yes, set up an appointment to discuss your interests, but be sure to do your homework on the topic first. List for yourself the questions you want to ask, and then take notes during the interview.

Other Print Resources in the Library

A great many print resources are available in libraries, including dictionaries and other reference sources. There are, for example, slang dictionaries that can tell you the history of rhyming slang, African-American slang, pig Latin, and so forth. If you are interested in information about people in the news or other prominent people, you can look in *Current Biography* or *Who's Who.* If you want to know about famous Americans from the past, you can look in the *Dictionary of American Biography* or *Who Was Who in America.* The

Dictionary of National Biography tells about men and women in British history. Librarians can point you to other works that you may find useful. Just remember that librarians are highly skilled in helping students find material. No matter how busy the librarian looks, you should not be intimidated. Do not be afraid to approach a librarian for help in finding resource material; that is the librarian's main purpose.

For example, we mentioned the *Annual Review of Psychology,* which is available in full text on InfoTrac College Edition and is also available in print. This is a serial publication (that is, one published at regular intervals) that provides in-depth articles on just about every subject in science, each article consisting of a detailed review by leading authorities on a specialized topic. Looking in the reference section of the *Annual Review of Psychology,* for example, can be a good way to find key studies. Other useful resources in psychology are called *handbooks;* if you search on this term in your library's automated catalog, you are likely to find several specialized handbooks. These edited books also contain detailed reviews, and although the emphasis of handbook chapters tends to be more idiosyncratic than the *Annual Review* or the articles in encyclopedias, perusing several of these resources can help you formulate an overall picture of the particular area of research in which you are interested.

Some journals also specialize in integrative reviews. One of these is the highly respected *Psychological Bulletin* (a bimonthly publication of the APA). Another excellent one is the *Review of General Psychology* (a quarterly journal of the APA's Division of General Psychology). Two other highly regarded journals, *Psychological Review* (a quarterly APA journal) and *Behavioral and Brain Sciences* (a quarterly published by Cambridge University Press), are other influential sources of integrative articles. One special feature of *Behavioral and Brain Sciences* is that, after each article, there is a section ("Open Peer Commentary") where you will find lively commentary on the article by other authors. The American Psychological Society (APS) publishes a supplement to its research journal *(Psychological Science),* called *Psychological Science in the Public Interest;* this is a semiannual monograph focusing on a single topic of public interest. For example, some of the topics covered in *Psychological Science in the Public Interest* are the influence of media violence on youth (December 2003), the role of self-esteem in happiness and health (May 2003), and the treatment and prevention of depression (November 2002). Another useful APS publication is *Current Directions in Psychology,* which contains summary integrative reviews of recent research findings in psychology. There are also a great many specialty review journals, such as the *Personality and Social Psychology Review.*

Taking Notes in the Library

We have discussed retrieving abstracts and other material online and locating original material in the stacks, but not taking notes in the library. If you have the funds, the best way to ensure that your notes will be exact is to photocopy the material you need. But be sure to write down in a conspicuous place on the photocopy the complete citation of all you copied. You will still need to interpret what you copied, and it is often easier to make notes of your interpretation at the time you have the material in hand. Having such notes will enable you to write an accurate paper as well as one that is efficiently organized.

Making detailed notes will also help you avoid committing *plagiarism* accidentally. We will have more to say about this problem later in this book, but you plagiarize intentionally when you knowingly copy or summarize someone's work without acknowledging the source. You plagiarize accidentally when you copy someone's work but forget to credit it or to put it in quotation marks. Plagiarism is illegal, and you should guard against it by keeping accurate notes and giving full credit to others when it is due.

If you are taking extensive notes on a laptop computer, you need some way to distance yourself from pages and pages of notes in order to bring coherence to them. The same would be true if you were taking handwritten notes in the library. A useful strategy with handwritten notes is to use a separate index card for each idea that you find as you uncover relevant material in your literature search. Many writers prefer making notes on large index cards because they can usually get all the information they want on the front of a large card, so it is easier to find what they want later. If you are using a computer to take notes, you can print them out and cluster them in logical batches (as you would large index cards). For each note, be sure to include the full reference of the material, including all the information you will need for the reference section of your paper, as well as the page numbers of verbatim quotes (to cite in the narrative of your paper).

If you have made an outline for a literature review (as described in Chapter Five), you can code each card or printout with the particular section of the outline that the material on the card or printout will illustrate (or you can use color coding). An alternative is to use a folder for each section of your paper, and then to file the relevant batches in the appropriate folder. In this way, you can maintain a general order in your notes and avoid facing a huge stack of miscellaneous bits and pieces of information that will loom large as you try to sort and integrate them into a useful form. If you are using reference numbers to code material, be consistent, because a haphazard arrangement will only slow you down when it is time to write the first draft.

The most fundamental rule of note taking is to be thorough and systematic so that you do not waste time and energy having to return to the same book or article. Because memory is porous, it is better to photocopy or record too much than to rely on recall to fill in the gaps. Be sure your notes will make sense to you when you examine them later.

Source Credibility

Not all information is reliable, but the question is how to separate the credible from the suspect. This question is not easy to answer: Two people may not perceive the same sources of information as credible. The way this problem is addressed in science is to subject manuscripts submitted to respected research journals to *peer review;* that is, the editors send the manuscripts to experts in the same field for independent evaluations and recommendations. It is not impossible for a poorly executed study to slip by occasionally, but as a general rule, researchers are taught to give greater weight to peer-reviewed journal articles than to unpublished manuscripts, technical reports, or chapters in edited books (which may be lightly reviewed, if at all). Textbooks are sent out for review, but mostly because the prospective publisher wants to find out whether they will be suitable for sale.

Even within the peer-reviewed literature, there is a pecking order of journals in any field. Manuscripts that are rejected by one journal might be sent to a second or third journal, until they finally find homes. This does not mean that articles in journals at the top of the pecking order are automatically more credible than those in other journals, only that a social hierarchy of journals exists in every field, and the toughest journals in which to publish are usually those at the top of the social structure. In some cases, 85% or more of manuscripts submitted to the most prestigious journals are rejected by the editors based on peer reviews, although some manuscripts may be returned without review because in the editor's judgment they seemed to be inappropriate for that particular journal. Yale psychologist Robert J. Sternberg wisely cautioned that "the place of publication is not a valid proxy for the quality and impact of the research" (*APA Observer,* October 2001, p. 40).

Some information is especially suspect, however, such as that in chat rooms on the Web. There is, in fact, a growing literature in psychological science on the nature of these chat rooms and the fertile ground they provide for rumor and gossip to take root. Because in a given instance it might be hard to decide whether something you read is a fact or a rumor (i.e., an unsupported allegation) or maybe even a bald-faced lie, the saying about "buying a pig in a poke" is applicable to much of this information. The best advice we can give you is: When in doubt, ask your instructor for guidance.

Additional Tips

As you get started on the literature search, try to be realistic in assessing how much material you will need in your review. Too few journal articles or books may result in a weak foundation for your project, but too much material and intemperate expectations may overwhelm you and your topic. You are writing not a doctoral dissertation or an article for a journal but a required paper that must be completed within a limited amount of time. How can you find out what is a happy medium between too little and too much? Talk with your instructor before you start an intensive literature search. Ask whether your plan seems realistic.

Here are some more tips to get you started on an efficient literature search:

- ♦ Ask the instructor to recommend any key works that you should read or consult. Even if you feel confident about your topic already, asking the instructor for specific leads can prevent your going off on a tangent.

- Do not expect to finish your literature search in one sitting. Students with unrealistic expectations make themselves overly anxious and rush a task that should be done patiently and methodically to achieve the best result.
- Suppose you cannot locate the original work that you are looking for in the stacks. Some students return repeatedly to the library, day after day, seeking a book or journal article before discovering that it has been lost or stolen or is being rebound. Ask an information librarian to find the elusive material. If the original work you need is unavailable, the librarian may consult another college library. However, the material could take so long to arrive that you might miss the deadline set by your instructor (this kind of delay is not an acceptable excuse).
- If you are looking for a specialized work, you probably will not find it in a small public library, so do not waste your time. When students spend a lot of time off-campus in public libraries and bookstores looking for source material, they usually come back with references from general texts or current mass-market books and periodicals, and these rarely constitute acceptable sources.
- Remember to keep a running checklist of the sources you searched and the search terms you used so that you don't accidentally retrace your steps.

Library Etiquette

Before we turn to the basics of developing your proposal for a review paper or a research project, here is some final advice about using your library. The golden rule of library etiquette is to respect your library and remember that others also have to use it:

- Be quiet.
- Never tear pages out of journals or books.
- Never write in library journals or books.
- Do not monopolize material or machines.
- Return books and periodicals as soon as you finish with them.

3

DEVELOPING
A PROPOSAL

*Once you have chosen your topic, retrieved background
information, and crystallized your ideas, the next step is to
develop a proposal. Some instructors feel that an oral
presentation is sufficient, but most require a written proposal to
ensure that both they and their students have the same
understanding of the topic and the planned project, including all
ethical issues in proposed research studies.*

Object of the Proposal

The object of your proposal is to tell the instructor what you would like to
study. However, it is not a one-way communication, but an opportunity for
the instructor to provide feedback and to raise questions that you need to address before going any further. If your assignment is an empirical research
study, the proposal is also an opportunity to anticipate and address any potential ethical concerns. You might think of the research proposal as a kind of
"letter of agreement" between you and the instructor. Once the research proposal has been approved, it is presumed that you will consult with the instructor before making changes in any aspect of the procedure. A proposal
for a literature review usually allows more flexibility. From it, the instructor
should be able to see whether you may be embarking on too grand a review
for the limited time available. It would be unreasonable to expect that you already know what you will conclude, although you probably have preliminary
ideas that you can express about the direction of your literature review.

Instructors may require submissions in addition to a written proposal,
and they may ask for details besides those in the sample proposals in this
chapter. In these sample proposals, the students are responding to the instructors' questions about how the idea for the project originated and why the
topic is worth studying. The purpose of such questions is (a) to stimulate you

to formulate plans, (b) to encourage you to choose a topic you find intrinsically interesting, and (c) to make sure that these are your own ideas. We will have more to say about the third point later in this book, but it is absolutely essential that the work be your own even if it builds on, or is a replication of, previous work by others.

In fact, replication is regarded as an essential criterion of credible scientific knowledge because it continues the discovery process of science as it clarifies and expands the meanings and limits of theories, hypotheses, and observations. Someone once compared the scientist to a person trying to unlock a door using a hitherto untried key. The role of replication, we might say, is to make the "key" available to others so they can see for themselves whether or not it works in a particular situation. This does not mean merely reproducing a similar p value. Instead, it means observing a similar relationship or phenomenon. Suppose you were out jogging and spotted two Martians—not two people disguised as Martians, but real Martians: green skin, antennas poking out of their scalps, and all the rest. You are not going to boot up your computer or whip out your calculator to run a significance test, but you sure are going to ask the nearest earthling, "Do you see what I see?"

Replications are sometimes the basis of senior theses and course projects. However, the student is expected to add a creative touch to the design, usually in the form of a new hypothesis or some other innovative aspect. For example, if the study you are replicating used two levels of the independent variable, you might experiment with three or four levels to find out whether there is a linear or a curvilinear relationship between the independent and dependent variables. If you can think of a moderator variable that might alter the relationship between the independent and dependent variables, then you can design a replication around your idea. Or you might choose a different measure of the dependent variable to see whether the original results are generalizable to more than one measure. Of course, you will want to design your study in a way that duplicates (as closely as possible) the original study even while you are investigating your own innovative addition; otherwise, you will find yourself in a logical bind if you need to explain any discrepancies between your results and the earlier study's. In writing the proposal for a replication study, it is a good idea to tell how you plan to compare the results. Do you propose a quantitative comparison of effect sizes or a qualitative analysis based on theoretically relevant characteristics, or perhaps a combination of both?

The Literature Review Proposal

Exhibit 10 illustrates one form of the kind of information that is generally reported in a proposal for a literature review. Although your instructor may ask you for some other information or require a different format, this exhibit will at least get you thinking about what usually belongs in a proposal for a review paper. It is clear that John's ideas did not come out of the blue; he met

EXHIBIT 10 *Sample proposal for a literature review*

John Smith 1

Proposal for a Literature Review for Psych 222

John Smith (e-mail address or other contact information)

(Date the proposal is submitted)

Working Title of Proposed Review

Comparison of Two Broad Theoretical Views of Intelligence

Objective of the Proposed Review

In Dr. Skleder's lecture on intelligence, she mentioned that she had done research on interpersonal acumen and that this research was inspired by the work of Howard Gardner. I have begun to read Gardner's work, and my preliminary understanding is that it is part of a movement away from the traditional view of intelligence. In the traditional view, the idea was that there is a common factor (called the *g* factor) in all of the standard measures of intelligence and IQ. The new movement, however, takes the position that there are many different kinds of intelligence within the same culture, a view that I am tentatively thinking of calling the *multiplex view.* Although there are a number of well-known proponents of the multiplex view, I plan to focus my literature review on Gardner's work and contrast it with the traditional *g*-centered view. I want to get a better understanding of both broad views of intelligence and the implications and limitations of each.

Literature Search Strategy

I plan to use PsycINFO to get started in my literature search, but I will also use some other possibly relevant databases, such as ERIC and InfoTrac. I anticipate that most of my reading will be concentrated on Gardner's books, and he has apparently written a lot. Because of time constraints, I can expect to read only a few of

EXHIBIT 10 *Continued*

John Smith 2

Gardner's publications, but I am also interested in reading the work of two other noted researchers in the multiplex area: Robert Sternberg and Steven Ceci. Inasmuch as the instructor has also done research in this area, I will confer with her about other possible sources of information. For example, she mentioned that some work has been done extending her earlier findings to managerial interpersonal acumen, and I will track down that follow-up research and at least cite it in the context of my discussion of current and possibly future directions.

I have done a preliminary search of textbook citations and a perusal of journal articles, and on the basis of this search, I identified an article by an American Psychological Association task force on "knowns and unknowns" about intelligence (Neisser et al., 1996). I have also found several books of Gardner's in the college library (Gardner, 1983, 1991, 1993), but I understand that he has written more since these appeared. There were some books by Ceci (1990) and Sternberg (1990; Sternberg & Detterman, 1986; Sternberg & Wagner, 1986) and two classic works of Thurstone's (1938; Thurstone & Thurstone, 1941) that a librarian helped me to locate in the dusty archives. Incidentally, another book that she recommended as relevant, but that is currently checked out (I have requested it), is Herrnstein and Murray's *The Bell Curve* (1994). These sources and Dr. Skleder's research article (Rosnow, Skleder, Jaeger, & Rind, 1994) appear in the preliminary list of references.

Preliminary List of References

Ceci, S. J. (1990). *On intelligence . . . more or less: A bioecological treatise on intellectual development*. Englewood Cliffs, NJ: Prentice Hall.

Gardner, H. (1983). *Frames of mind: The theory of multiple intelligences*. New York: Basic Books.

EXHIBIT 10 *Continued*

John Smith 3

Gardner, H. (1991). *The unschooled mind: How children think and how schools should teach.* New York: Basic Books.

Gardner, H. (1993). *Multiple intelligences: The theory in practice.* New York: Basic Books.

Herrnstein, R. J., & Murray, C. (1994). *The bell curve: Intelligence and class structure in American life.* New York: Free Press.

Neisser, U., Boodoo, G., Bouchard, T. J., Jr., Boykin, A. W., Brody, N., Ceci, S. J., Halpern, D. F., Loehlin, J. C., Perloff, R., Sternberg, R. J., & Urbina, S. (1996). Intelligence: Knowns and unknowns. *American Psychologist, 51,* 77–101.

Rosnow, R. L., Skleder, A. A., Jaeger, M. E., & Rind, B. (1994). Intelligence and the epistemics of interpersonal acumen: Testing some implications of Gardner's theory. *Intelligence, 19,* 93–116.

Sternberg, R. J. (1990). *Metaphors of mind: A new theory of human intelligence.* New York: Cambridge University Press.

Sternberg, R. J., & Detterman, D. K. (Eds.). (1986). *What is intelligence? Contemporary viewpoints on its nature and definition.* Norwood, NJ: Ablex.

Sternberg, R. J., & Wagner, R. K. (Eds.). (1986). *Practical intelligence: Nature and origins of competence in the everyday world.* New York: Cambridge University Press.

Thurstone, L. L. (1938). *Primary mental abilities.* Chicago: University of Chicago Press.

Thurstone, L. L., & Thurstone, T. G. (1941). *Factorial studies of intelligence.* (Psychometric Society Psychometric Monographs No. 2). Chicago: University of Chicago Press.

with the instructor even before drafting this proposal in order to get preliminary feedback. He got his initial idea from the instructor's lecture and soon afterward began to look up relevant references. The "multiplex view" that John mentions and defines in the proposal is his own idea for how he wants to approach the project. He has an impressive preliminary list of references, but he notes that he plans to use PsycINFO and other relevant databases "to get started" in his literature search. That John and the instructor have a mutual interest in the topic will be a boon to John as he pursues the "follow-up research" mentioned by the instructor.

Regarding the format of the proposal, notice that John's name is typed above each page beside the page number; this identification will serve as a safety device if any pages get accidentally detached. Some instructors prefer that students insert a page header (a couple of words from the title), like the page headers in the final review paper in Appendix B. John shows his e-mail address or other contact information, making it easy for the instructor to communicate with John. The title is called a *working title* to reflect the idea that it can be changed later and is meant only to give an overall preview at this point. After describing the intention or goal of John's projected review and his plan for retrieving information, the proposal concludes with the preliminary list of references formatted in APA style. The proposal is written in a way that indicates that John has already put a lot of effort into the project.

The Research Proposal

Exhibit 11 illustrates one form of a proposal for a research project. Jane begins by telling how she came up with her idea and what preliminary work she has done. Particularly impressive is that after getting the instructor's tentative OK, she found a restaurant where she could run the study. She has already informed the restaurant owner and the server about the nature of her proposed research and gotten their written approval to show to the instructor. Thus, once her proposal has been approved, Jane will be able to get started. Jane's discussion of hypotheses and predictions is precise, another indication that she has already done a lot of work. The more thorough Jane is, the more focused the instructor's comments can be in shepherding Jane toward her goal. If you plan to develop a questionnaire, put a preliminary verbal sketch of it in the proposal so the instructor can give you feedback with specific suggestions.

Jane also gives a sense of how her results might be analyzed, but she mentions that she has "not yet settled on the particular data analysis." She does, however, give a clear idea of how the dependent variable will be defined, and she shows that she perceives how the data analysis must address her predictions. After discussing the ethics of the research, Jane lists all the studies cited in the proposal. The level of detail reflects the considerable amount of time that Jane has already spent, as well as her consultations with the instructor on more than one occasion.

EXHIBIT 11 *Sample proposal for a research study*

Jane Doe 1

Research Proposal for Psych 333

Jane Doe (e-mail address or other contact information)

(Date the proposal is submitted)

Working Title of Proposed Research

An Experimental Investigation of the Effects of a Small Gift on Restaurant Tipping

Objective of the Research

In a lecture, Dr. Rind mentioned the field experiments he has done on tipping behavior (Rind & Bordia, 1995, 1996). I am interested in this work not only theoretically, but also because I have a summer job as a waitress. Dr. Rind also mentioned an article by Lynn (1996), which got me further interested in the techniques that servers can use to stimulate tipping. Many of the techniques described by Lynn seemed to involve boosting customers' impressions of the server's friendliness (e.g., a friendly touch or drawing a smiling face on the check). I propose to experiment with another technique, described below. After first discussing my idea with the instructor in a very preliminary way, and getting his approval to proceed to the next stage, I asked an acquaintance who owns a restaurant for permission to perform a study in which the server will present customers with a small gift (chocolate candy). The objective of this research will be to investigate whether the techniques that are described here can be used to improve tipping behavior. They are all based on the interaction between the server and the customers when the check is presented, but in particular the server's offer of a token gift (candy) when the check is presented. Attached to this proposal are signed written permissions I received from the restaurant owner and the server who will participate in this study.

Hypotheses and Predictions

I have also read an article by Regan (1971) and have become interested in whether reciprocity (i.e., the idea that people feel obligated to return a favor) may

EXHIBIT 11 *Continued*

Jane Doe 2

further improve the effectiveness of the technique I propose to use. Specifically, I propose to manipulate this condition by having the server say, in an offhand manner, "Oh, have another piece of candy," which should create the impression that the candy favor is due to the server's (as opposed to the restaurant's) generosity. My hypothesis is that customers in this treatment condition will feel obligated to return the server's favor by increasing the tips they give.

Altogether, I propose three hypotheses, which proceed on the assumption that the server's offer of candy will be perceived by customers as a gesture of friendliness. My first hypothesis is that the mere offer of the candy will have the effect of increasing tips when compared with a no-gift control condition. Second, I hypothesize that this effect is cumulative, so that offering two candies should stimulate tipping even more (compared with the control). Third, proceeding from Regan's description of reciprocity, I hypothesize that creating the impression that the server is generous (as well as friendly) should elicit the most tipping.

Proposed Method

The restaurant is an upscale Italian-American establishment in central New Jersey. I have gotten the owner's permission and have also described the proposed study to a female server, who has agreed to participate. I propose using a randomized design with the following four groups: (a) no candy condition, (b) 1 piece of candy condition, (c) 2 pieces of candy condition, and (d) 1+1 condition. I will write the condition on a card, shuffle the cards, and ask the server to draw (blindly) one card at a time. In the control condition, the instruction will be to present the check without any candy. In the 1-piece condition, the instruction will be to offer each customer in the dining party one piece of candy when presenting the check. In the 2-piece condition, the instruction will be to offer each customer two pieces of candy of the person's choice when presenting the check. In the 1+1 condition, the instruction will be to offer each customer one piece of candy and then say, "Oh, have another piece," as if it were a generous afterthought.

EXHIBIT 11 *Continued*

Jane Doe 3

The server's interaction with customers in the dining party will be limited to taking their orders, bringing them their food, presenting the check, and following the instructions on the randomly selected card. When the dining party leaves, the server will record privately on the same index card that was used to specify the treatment (a) the amount of the tip left by the party, (b) the amount of the bill before taxes, and (c) the party size. It should be possible to run 20 dining parties in each condition. This process will give me an equal number of cases (n) in each condition, which is preferable to an unequal-n design because the more unequal the groups are, the less is the statistical power relative to an equal-n design with the same total sample size (N). In setting $N = 80$, I am assuming that this number will provide enough statistical power for me to detect medium-sized effects (r approximately .3) using t tests to compare conditions. However, as I have no empirically-based idea of the magnitude of the anticipated effect, this total N is a guess, but I am hoping it is a reasonable number given the limited time available to conduct this research. Afterward, however, I plan to use Cohen's (1992) power primer to make an estimate of the effective power.

Proposed Data Analysis

The dependent measure will be defined as the tip percentage—that is, the amount of the tip divided by the amount of the bill before taxes, which will then be multiplied by 100. I will begin by examining the basic descriptive data (means and variabilities), but I have not yet settled on the particular data analyses I will use to evaluate the hypotheses, as there are several possibilities based on the text. One possibility is to run t tests comparing each experimental group with the control, in which case I predict that the effect size (r) will be largest for the comparison of the 1+1 condition with the control condition and smallest for the comparison of the 1-piece condition with the control condition. In my initial meeting with Dr. Rind, he suggested another possibility to test my overall prediction, which is to compute a linear contrast F. I will need to do some further reading before tackling this

EXHIBIT 11 *Continued*

Jane Doe 4

approach, but the idea would be to perform a contrast analysis on all four conditions, which will allow me to evaluate the predicted increase in tipping from control to 1-piece to 2-piece to 1+1 conditions.

Ethical Considerations

The study involves a mild deception in that the customers are unaware that they are participating in an experiment. I do not propose to debrief them because no potential risk is involved. I cannot ask people who are dining whether they will agree to "participate in an experiment," because that would destroy the credibility of the manipulation and render the results scientifically meaningless. The server and the owner will be given full details of the results, and all tips will be the property of the server.

Preliminary List of References

Cohen, J. (1992). A power primer. *Psychological Bulletin, 112,* 155–159.

Lynn, M. (1996). Seven ways to increase servers' tips. *Cornell Hotel and Restaurant Administration Quarterly, 37*(3), 24–29.

Regan, D. T. (1971). Effects of a favor and liking on compliance. *Journal of Experimental Social Psychology, 7,* 627–639.

Rind, B., & Bordia, P. (1995). Effect of server's "thank you" and personalization on restaurant tipping. *Journal of Applied Social Psychology, 25,* 745–751.

Rind, B., & Bordia, P. (1996). Effect of restaurant tipping of male and female servers drawing a happy, smiling face on the backs of customers' checks. *Journal of Applied Social Psychology, 26,* 218–225.

Ethical Considerations

Jane's discussion of ethics is brief; other proposals may call for a more detailed ethics discussion. Jane may also be asked to provide a stronger rationale for her "mild deception" or to provide other relevant information. The reason for requiring a detailed discussion is that ethical accountability is important in every aspect of research. The absolute requirements of ethical accountability are (a) that you, the researcher, will protect the dignity, privacy, and safety of your subjects; (b) that your study will be technically sound (so as not to waste precious resources, including the subjects' time and effort); and (c) that your study will not be detrimental to society.

Here are some specific questions to get you thinking about the ethics of your proposed study:

◆ Might there be any psychological or physical risks to the subjects? How do you plan to avoid these risks?
◆ Will any deception be used, and if so, is it really necessary, or can you think of a way to avoid deception?
◆ How do you plan to debrief the subjects? If you really must use a deception, then how do you plan to "dehoax" the deceived subjects? How can you be sure that the dehoaxing procedure was effective?
◆ How do you plan to recruit the subjects, and can you be sure that the recruitment procedure is noncoercive?
◆ How do you plan to use informed consent and to ensure that the subjects understand that they are free to withdraw at any time without penalty?
◆ What steps will you take to ensure the confidentiality of the data?

Tempus Fugit

Because time flies when you are writing a required paper, here are two final tips:

◆ Turn in your proposal on time. Instructors are also very busy people, and they (like you) schedule their work. Turning in a proposal late signals the wrong message to your instructor. Instead of communicating that you are responsible and reliable and someone who thinks clearly, the red flag of a late proposal signals that you may be none of the above.
◆ Be precise. In Lewis Carroll's *Through the Looking Glass,* Alice (*Alice in Wonderland*) comes upon Humpty Dumpty, who uses a word in a way that Alice says she does not understand. He smiles contemptuously and says, "Of course you don't—till I tell you. . . . When *I* use a word, it means just what I choose it to mean—neither more nor less." Unlike Humpty Dumpty, you do not have the luxury of telling your instructor to "take it or leave it." Nor do you have the extra time to keep resubmitting the proposal because you did not make the initial effort to be precise.

4

PLANNING THE RESEARCH REPORT

The basic structure and form of research reports in psychology have evolved over many years. In this chapter, we describe this structure in the context of the sample report in Appendix A. Familiarity with these matters will enable you to organize your thoughts and plan the first draft. (If you are writing a review paper, you can skip this chapter and go on to Chapter Five.)

Three Broad Research Approaches

Research methods texts routinely cover data collection and data analysis, and we will assume that you are mastering those techniques (though we have more to say about reporting statistical information in Chapter Six). What primarily remains is developing a research report that will explain in clear language (a) what you did, (b) why you did it, (c) what you found out, (d) what your findings mean, and (e) what you have concluded. Research methods texts usually make fine distinctions among the kinds of research strategies, such as the laboratory experiment, the sample survey, the case study, and the archival approach. The study reported by Jane Doe in Appendix A illustrates another strategy, an experiment in a field setting. Over and above these fine differences is another distinction among three broad research approaches: the descriptive, the relational, and the experimental. Each of these has its own objective, reflected in the answers that would be given to the five questions above.

The usual purpose of descriptive research in human psychology is to map out an aspect of how people feel, think, or behave. As an example, a student in educational psychology might describe the behavior of failing pupils in a particular school. The student's report of her empirical findings will describe how she (and perhaps others) sat in on classes and observed and recorded the behavior of the pupils. She might propose theoretical ideas or discuss ideas for further research, but the primary focus of her research report will be on describing as carefully as possible what she observed and measured, and what she has concluded.

Sooner or later, however, someone will want to know *how* what happens behaviorally is related to other variables. The how is the object of the relational research approach, which is an examination of how certain variables are related or how the behavior of interest is correlated with certain events. An example might be a correlational study of the association between children's failure in school and (a) whether the children were learning and (b) the degree to which the teacher had been exposing the children to the material to be learned. The research report would examine the relationship between (b) and (a)—that is, the amount of the children's exposure to the material to be learned and the amount of material that the children learned. The researcher would indicate not just whether (a) and (b) are significantly related (i.e., whether, over the long run, this nonzero relationship is likely to emerge consistently if the research is repeated), but also the form of the relationship (e.g., linear or nonlinear, positive or negative) and the magnitude of the relationship, or the effect size.

The third broad type, the experimental approach, is focused more on the identification of determining factors, or causes (i.e., how things get to be the way they are, or what leads to what). Relational research can only rarely provide such insights, and then only under very special conditions. We will have more to say about the language of "causality" in a later chapter, but it is important when writing a relational research report not to use any language that implies causality—that is, the idea that (a) is *responsible* for (b). Randomized drug trials in biomedical research are one example of the experimental approach, as is Jane Doe's study of tipping behavior in Appendix A (using randomization to assign dining parties to the four conditions). Some scientific researchers use the term *experiment* simply to mean "to test" or "to try," as when Galileo imagined dropping objects of different weights from the Leaning Tower of Pisa to test his prediction that they would land at the same time. In psychology, a behaviorist's example of a "single-case experiment" might be a report of how a child's failure behavior was extinguished when proper behavioral techniques were followed by the teacher.

The Basic Structure

Whether a report describes descriptive, relational, or experimental research, a well-written paper implies a logical progression in thought. By adhering to the structure described in the remainder of this chapter, you can create this kind of order in your finished paper. It is, of course, possible, that the nature of your research may require a deviation from this basic structure. For example, if you were reporting more than one study, you might find it preferable to discuss each study in turn rather than lump them together in a single method section or a single results section. It is rare that students actually have the time to conduct more than one study for a course requirement, but the point is that this basic structure is not carved in stone. If you feel that you must deviate from it, confer with the instructor beforehand.

The basic structure of most research reports in psychology consists of the following eight parts, as illustrated by Jane's report:

Title page
Abstract
Introduction
Method
Results
Discussion
References
End material (tables and appendix)

Except for the layout of the title page and the addition of an appendix in Jane's paper, her structure corresponds to a standard reporting format that has evolved over many years, and it is also typical of what you will see when you read research reports in psychology journals. Later on, we will discuss the layout of the paper, but you can see that the title page is straightforward, so let us focus on the parts that remain.

Abstract

Although the abstract (or synopsis) appears at the beginning of your report, it is actually written after the paper is completed. The abstract provides a concise summary of your report. Think of it as a distillation into one succinct paragraph of the important points covered in the body of the report. In the sample research report, Jane summarizes what she did, what she found, and what she concluded.

When planning your abstract, answer these questions as concisely as possible:

♦ What was the objective or purpose of my research study?
♦ What principal method did I use?
♦ Who were the research participants?
♦ What were my major findings?
♦ What did I conclude from these findings?

More detailed and more specific statements about methods, results, and conclusions are given in the body of your report. The abstract is presented first, and its purpose is to let the reader anticipate what your report is about.

Introduction

The introduction provides the rationale for your research and prepares the reader for the methods you have chosen. Thus, you should give a concise history and background of your topic, leading into your hypotheses or questions. That is, you are using an evidence-based argument to explain the objective or purpose of your research study and what you predicted. Stating something on the order of "X (1990) reported an effect of study time, but this experiment was criticized by Y (1992) for methodological flaws" would not be good evidence-based writing. The reason is that it fails to adequately describe the effect reported by researcher X and does not identify the methodological flaws identified by researcher Y. Nor would it be acceptable to present merely a string of loosely related summaries of articles, because you need to show that you understand what you are citing and how it supports a particular position.

In her opening paragraph, Jane presents a demographic finding and its implications for the importance of her topic. In this way, she develops an evidence-based argument underscoring the value of her research and the logical foundation of her hypotheses. The following paragraphs pick up the thread from the first paragraph. Jane describes succinctly, but in precise detail, what was found in the research she cites. Some students tend to simply assert conclusions advocated by the authors of cited studies and fail to describe the evidence the researchers used to support those assertions. Jane, however, deftly leads into her three hypotheses; she takes nothing for granted and instead walks the reader step-by-step through the reasoning behind each hypothesis.

Your literature review should also show the development of your hypotheses or any of your exploratory questions and the reason(s) the research topic seemed worth studying. Strong introductions are those that state the research problem or the hypotheses in such a way that the method section appears to be a natural consequence of that statement. If you can get the readers to think when they later see your method section, "Yes, of course, that's what this researcher had to do to answer this question," then you will have succeeded in writing a strong introduction. Here are some questions to ask yourself as you plan the introduction:

- ◆ What was the purpose of my study?
- ◆ What terms need to be defined?
- ◆ How does my study build on or derive from other studies?
- ◆ What were my hypotheses, predictions, or expectations?

Method

The next step is to detail the methods and procedures used. The research participants should be described—for example, their age and sex. The number of people participating and the way they were selected or recruited also should be specified. Psychologists are trained to ask questions about the generalizability of results. Your instructor will be thinking about the generalizability of your findings across both persons and settings (referred to as the *external validity* of the study). If your subjects were college students, think about how your results can be generalized beyond this specialized population (and discuss these ideas later in your report).

Also included in this section should be a description of any tests or measures and the context in which they were used. Even if you used well-known, standardized tests, it is still a good idea to describe them in a few sentences. By describing them, you tell the instructor that you understand the nature and purpose of the measuring instruments you used.

For instance, suppose you used the Self-Monitoring Scale developed by psychologist Mark Snyder (see "Self Monitoring of Expressive Behavior," *Journal of Personality and Social Psychology*, 1974, vol. 30, pp. 526–537). In your literature search, you found that research has shown this instrument to be three-dimensional (see "An Analysis of the Self-Monitoring Scale," by S. R. Briggs, J. M. Cheek, and A. H. Buss, *Journal of Personality and Social Psychology*, 1980, vol. 38, pp. 679–686). In your report, you might say something like:

> The study participants were administered Snyder's (1974) 25-item Self-Monitoring Scale. The original purpose of this instrument was to measure self-control and self-observation, but Briggs, Cheek, and Buss (1980) found that the scale actually measures three distinct factors, described by them as extraversion, other-directedness, and acting. *Extraversion* refers to the tendency to be the center of attention in groups; *other-directedness,* to a person's willingness to change his or her behavior to suit others; and *acting,* to liking and being good at speaking and entertaining.

However, suppose you need to report only the nature of a particular measure and not any follow-up inferences by other researchers. For example, assume you used the Need for Cognition Scale created by social psychologists John T. Cacioppo and Richard E. Petty (see "The Need for Cognition," *Journal of Personality and Social Psychology*, 1982, vol. 42, pp. 116–131). You can succinctly describe the measure in a single sentence:

> The participants were administered Cacioppo and Petty's (1982) Need for Cognition Scale, which is an 18-item measure of the tendency to engage in and enjoy thinking.

If you know something about the reliability and validity of the instrument, mention this information as well (along with an appropriate citation), but be specific. It would be vague to say only that "the reliability was $r = .50$" without also indicating whether you mean the *test-retest reliability* (the stability of the instrument from one measurement session to another), the *alternate form reliability* (the degree of equivalence of different versions of the instrument), or the *internal-consistency reliability* (the degree of relatedness of individual items or components of the instrument when those items or components are used to give a single score). The same rule applies to the reporting of validity findings; tell which type of validity you mean of those described in Exhibit 12.

EXHIBIT 12   Uses of the term *validity* in research and assessment

---

construct validity: the degree to which the conceptual variable (or construct) that is presumably measured or studied is what is claimed.

content validity: the adequate sampling of the relevant material or content that a test purports to measure.

criterion validity: the degree to which a measuring instrument is correlated with outcome criteria in the present (its *concurrent validity*) or the future (its *predictive validity*).

ecological validity: the adequacy of an experimental research design in sampling subjects and stimuli.

external validity: the generalizability of an inferred causal relationship over different people, settings, manipulations, and research outcomes.

face validity: the degree to which a measuring instrument "looks as if" it is measuring something relevant.

internal validity: the soundness of statements about whether one variable is responsible for (i.e., the cause of) a particular outcome.

statistical-conclusion validity: the accuracy of drawing certain statistical conclusions, such as statistical significance or an estimation of the effect size.

Results

In the next major section, describe your findings. You might plan to show the results in a table, as in Jane's report, or in a bar graph or other visual display. Do not make the reader guess what you are thinking; label your table or figure fully, and discuss the data in the narrative text so that it is clear what the results represent. It is not necessary to repeat every single result from the table or figure in your narrative; simply tell what the results mean. (We will have more to say about the use of visual displays in Chapter Six.)

Ask yourself the following questions as you structure your results section:

- What did I find?
- How can I say what I found in a careful, detailed way?
- Is what I am planning to say precise and to the point?
- Will what I have said be clear to the reader?
- Have I left out anything of importance?

We will have more to say in Chapter Six about precision in reporting statistical details, but a question that many students ask is how precise they should be in reporting test statistics (such as the t test, the F test, and the chi-square), effect sizes, measures of central tendency (such as means and medians), and measures of variability (standard deviations and variances). The rule of thumb is to round these statistics to two decimal places, as shown in the results section of Jane's report. But in calculating the results, it is essential not to scrimp on the number of decimal places in the intermediate calculations (as illustrated in the appendix of Jane's report, where she shows calculations).

Suppose you were an engineer at the National Aeronautics and Space Administration, and you were trying to figure out how much fuel would be needed to complete a manned mission to Mars. If you rounded the calculations, you might send the astronauts on an impossible mission.

Another convention that many students find confusing is the way that p values are to be presented. Many statisticians recommend reporting the actual descriptive level of significance, because it carries more information than the phrases "significant difference" and "no significant difference at the 5% level." Assuming your instructor does not frown on reporting p values in the narrative text to more than two or three decimal places, you have several options. One possibility is to list a string of zeros, such as "$p = .00000025$." An alternative (the one used by Jane) is to use scientific notation as a more compact way to show a very small p value. Instead of reporting $p = .00000025$, you report 2.5^{-7}, where -7 tells the reader to count 7 places to the left of the decimal in 2.5 and make that the decimal place. Of course, if you are looking up p values in a statistical table, you may not have the option of reporting them precisely in the narrative text. In this case, your only option may be to state that p is less than ($<$) or greater than ($>$) the particular column value in the statistical table. When correlations and certain statistical tests are reported in tables, the APA manual recommends that asterisks ordinarily be used to identify the probability values (as illustrated in Jane's Table 2).

Discussion

In the discussion section of your research report, you will form a cohesive unit from the facts you have gathered. Think about how you will discuss your findings in light of how your hypotheses were stated. But also describe any sudden insights or unexpected ideas you had. Incidentally, the name for a lucky discovery is *serendipity;* it is derived from a fairy tale about three princes of Serendip (an ancient name for Sri Lanka) who were constantly making lucky findings. For example, the invention of Velcro fasteners came about when a man, while picking cockleburs from his jacket after a stroll in the Swiss countryside, noticed that they were covered with hooks that had become embedded in the loops of the fabric of his jacket. Serendipity is quite common in everyday life (and also in science) when people keep an open mind that allows them to perceive things in novel ways.

Previously, we mentioned using an evidence-based argument when pulling studies together in the introduction section of your report. In the discussion section, you are now making another evidence-based argument, but this time you must try to write "defensively" without being too blatant about it. Be your own devil's advocate and ask yourself what a skeptical reader might see as the other side of your argument or conclusion. Are there shortcomings or inconsistencies, and how might a reader react? All research findings are limited in some ways, but if you cannot find any holes in your argument or conclusion, ask a clever friend to help you out by listening to what you would like to argue or conclude in your discussion. Jane writes defensively about the statistical power of her study, in that she makes an evidence-based argument that it "was much lower than the recommended level of .80" but mentions that, in selecting the sample size, she "was limited by the fact that the research had to be conducted, analyzed, and reported by the end of the semester."

Here are some additional questions to consider as you begin to structure this section:

- What was the purpose of my study?
- How do my results relate to that purpose?
- Were there any serendipitous findings of interest?
- How valid and generalizable are my findings?
- Are there larger implications in these findings?
- Is there an alternative way to interpret my results?

If you believe your findings lead to practical or larger implications, the discussion is the place to spell them out. Are there implications for further research? Jane shows that she understands that replications are another way to improve statistical power—that is, by pooling the significance levels meta-analytically. In her final sentence, she alludes to the practical implication of her results in a charming, personal aside. Some researchers prefer to add a separate section, called "Conclusions," when they want to separate the ideas and arguments in the discussion from some pithy conclusions that need elaboration. This extra section is usually not necessary if all you have is one or two conclusions that you can state in the final paragraph of your discussion section. In either case, your conclusions should be stated as clearly, accurately, and precisely as possible.

References

Once you have made plans for writing the body of the report, think about your reference material again. You will need to include an alphabetized listing of all the sources of information you drew from, and it is essential that every article, chapter, and book (not personal communications) be listed in your references section. To avoid retracing your steps, it is good to keep a running list of the material that will appear in this section as you progress through the early preparation of the report. You can create a separate file called "References" and then copy and paste them into the paper's references section. If at the last minute you find you need to recheck the author, title, or publisher of a particular book, remember that you can go to your library's automated catalog.

End Material

The APA manual stipulates that tables and figures be placed in the manuscript after the references section, which is a convenience for the copyeditor and the printer. Jane's report adheres to this style, as many instructors prefer students use it. However, because your paper is not being submitted for publication, your instructor may permit you to insert tables and figures within the narrative text; this is easy enough to do if you are using a standard word-processing program. The APA manual adds that footnotes to the narrative text should be on a separate page immediately after the references section and before any tables or figures, another convenience for the printer of journal articles. Not all instructors insist on this format, and you should check with your instructor if you have a question about how to proceed (ask whether it is OK to let your word-processing program automatically insert footnotes at the bottom of relevant pages).

Most instructors like to see the raw materials and computations of the investigation. The information can be prepared as an appendix at the end of your report (as Jane's report illustrates) or, if the instructor prefers, as a separate package of materials. Had Jane used a test or questionnaire that did not belong in the limited space of the method section, she would have included it here in the appendix of her report. If you used a statistical program to analyze your data, you can make a printout, pare it down to essentials, and include the pared-down results as an appendix in your paper. Whether or not your instructor requires an appendix (or stipulates a different list of items to be included), it is very important that you keep all your notes and raw data until the instructor has returned your report and you have received a grade in the course—just in case the instructor has questions about your work.

Organizing Your Thoughts

In the next chapter we describe the way to create an outline for a review paper. The research report does not require a gross outline because its formal structure already provides a skeleton waiting to be fleshed out. Nevertheless, all researchers find it absolutely essential to organize their thoughts about each section before writing the first draft. There are three ways to do this:

◆ If you would like to learn about outlining, Chapter Five provides guidelines on how to outline before or after the fact.
◆ You can make notes on separate index cards for each major point (for example, the rationale of the study, the derivation of each hypothesis, and each background study) and draw on these notes to write your first draft.
◆ You can simply make a computer file of such notes.

If you are still having a hard time organizing your thoughts, try dictating your ideas into a tape recorder. Take the tape recorder for a walk, and tell it what you found in your research. Another possibility is to imagine you are sitting across a table from a friend; tell your "friend" what you found. No matter what approach you favor, make sure that your notes or files are accurate and complete. If you are summarizing or paraphrasing something you read, you must provide full information about the source. If you are quoting someone, include the statement in quotation marks and make sure that you have copied it exactly.

5

OUTLINING THE
REVIEW PAPER

*When you are ready to begin drafting your review paper, the first
step is to create a rough outline. The imposition of form will help
you collect and refine your thoughts as you shape the paper, and
you can prepare a more detailed outline after you have thought
some more. But even if you do not outline before you begin the
first draft, you should at least do so afterward. If a logical,
ordered form does not emerge, the weak spots will become
apparent and you can fix them.*

Where to Start

A weak structure or a lack of structure is a common flaw in students' literature
reviews and other term papers. There's a paragraph on X's study, and then one
on Y's study, and then another one on the study by Z, but as one instructor
complained, "My students' literature reviews often read like catalogs of studies with no real organization." A weak structure is a sure sign that the student
did not develop an outline before beginning to write—or even after drafting
the paper. Without at least a rough outline to work with, the first draft of the
paper can ramble on endlessly, and working with it is like shaking hands with
an octopus.

In contrast, if you have a rough outline, you know where your ideas and
sentences are heading. For example, you might organize the studies you
want to review in chronological order or group them by results that supported one hypothesis and then results that supported an alternative hypothesis, or you might organize them by methodological features. The more
effort you put into structuring your paper, the more coherent the final product will be and the more likely you are to complete it on time. In Appendix B,
John Smith details in the opening paragraph how his paper is organized.

It begins by contrasting two views of intelligence and mentioning their chronological development.

You can begin to organize studies into a tentative and general outline as you retrieve and read reference material. Use comparison and contrast as a way of categorizing them into groups and subgroups. Add or remove components as you pull together facts, arguments, and studies that document and expand your subtopics. Like a science fiction movie about an amorphous mass that gradually takes shape out of primordial ooze, the structure of even the most incoherent paper will inevitably acquire form and shape if you keep thinking about it patiently. Your organizing does not have to be done in one sitting, and in fact it is usually better to take a break, go for a walk, work on something else, and then come back to the problem with a refreshed mind.

Your objective is to produce a parallel construction and a balanced hierarchy of organization. However, if you find it difficult to begin making even a rough outline, there are two tricks you can try:

◆ Think of the outline as a very detailed table of contents based on the headings and subheadings you might want to use in a particular section of your paper.
◆ Shop around for an interesting quote that encourages fresh thinking, and if it still seems relevant later on, you can use it to launch the introduction as well as capture and focus the reader's interest.

Before attempting the first draft (discussed in Chapter Seven), you will need to revise and polish the preliminary outline so that it more precisely reflects the organizational structure of your paper. Even this structure should be viewed not as carved in stone, but as something that can be molded to your ideas as they evolve. Use the structure to guide you, but do not be afraid to change it if your thinking changes.

The Rough Outline

The first outline you do can be simply a numbered list of items you want to cover in your paper. You can then think about this list, put it aside for a day or so, and then think about it some more. Asking yourself the following questions should help you get going:

◆ How do I want to begin?
◆ What conclusions do I want to draw?
◆ What sections do I need between these two points?
◆ In each section, what do I want to emphasize?
◆ What illustrations, examples, or quotations can I use?
◆ What details do I use? In what order?

Turning again to John's paper, you can see that all these questions are addressed. If we could go back a couple of steps and ask how John began structuring his paper, we would find that he might have sketched something like this for his first rough draft:

1. Point out that "intelligence" has different meanings in different contexts, and conclude the introduction with an overview of the rest of the paper.
2. Compare the traditional view of intelligence with the newer view, which I'll be calling the *multiplex view* of intelligence.
3. Emphasize Gardner's theory of multiple intelligences, including his ideas on what defines a component of intelligence, what his seven kinds of intelligence are, and why he believes they are independent intellectual abilities.
4. Discuss the major criticisms of the newer view, and give some arguments that counter these criticisms.
5. End by rehashing the point of the paper, noting its limitations, and saying something about the current or future direction of research.

There is enough here for John to begin to think about the fine details of each section and to frame a more meticulous outline. In getting down to specifics, he needs to keep all of his ideas parallel to ensure that there will be logical consistency in his arguments. Just as the preliminary outline can take different forms, the detailed outline can be set down in topics, sentences, or paragraphs—whichever makes the most sense to you as your ideas begin to flow. The essential point is that these ideas are comparable or equivalent to one another—that is, parallel.

Making Ideas Parallel

Choose whether to use topics, sentences, or paragraphs for your outline; then use only the specific form you have chosen. In the following outline fragment, the ideas are clearly not parallel:

   I. What is intelligence? What does "*g*-centric" mean? What will follow?
  II. Two views
     A. Traditional—the general overriding factor of intelligence is measured by every task on an intelligence test
     B. Spearman's psychometric contribution
     C. Developmental psychologists, following Piaget, argue for general mental structures
     D. *The Bell Curve*

The problem is that this outline is a hodgepodge of questions, topics, idea fragments, and a book title. Working with this jumble would be like swimming upstream in your efforts to put thoughts and notes into a logical sequence.

Contrast that incoherent structure with the parallel structure of this beginning of an outline:

   I. Two views of intelligence
      A. The traditional approach
         1. General overriding trait (Spearman)
            a. "*g*-centric" notion of intelligence
            b. Jensen and heritability
         2. Piaget's idea of general structures of the mind
            a. Universal developmental sequence
            b. Biological operationalization (speed of neural transmission)
         3. Herrnstein and Murray's book on role of *g* in society

What makes the second outline fragment superior to the first is not only that the same form is used throughout but that, in the second outline, the ideas are also logically ordered. The second outline looks more polished and inviting and will certainly be easier to use as a writing plan.

Putting Ideas in Order

To create this polished look, whether you use topics, sentences, or paragraphs for your outline, the trick is to try to group your information in descending order, from the most general facts or ideas to the most specific details and examples. You can see this approach clearly in the parallel format of the outline shown immediately above.

The rule of orderly precision applies whether you are outlining definitions, the nature of a particular theory, evaluation criteria, or a series of arguments and counterarguments. You can see the order and precision in the following outline segment:

   II. Gardner's theory of "intelligences"
      A. Definition of intelligence
         1. Problem solving and creative abilities
         2. Evaluation criteria
            a. Isolation if brain-damaged
            b. Existence of exceptional populations
            c. Unique core operations
            d. Distinctive developmental history
            e. Existence of primitive antecedents
            f. Openness to experimentation
            g. Prediction of performance on tests
            h. Accessibility of information content
      B. Kinds of intelligence
         1. Logical-mathematical
         2. Linguistic

EXHIBIT 13   *Subdivision of the outline*

I.
   A.
   B.
      1.
      2.
         a.
         b.
            (1)
            (2)
               (a)
               (b)
II.

---

     3. Spatial
     4. Bodily-kinesthetic
     5. Musical
     6. Personal
        a. Intrapersonal
        b. Interpersonal

Another convention in making a detailed outline, as illustrated in Exhibit 13, is that if there is a subtopic division, there should be at least two subtopics, never only one. Facts, ideas, and concepts are classified by the use of roman numerals I, II, III; capitals A, B, C; arabic numerals 1, 2, 3; small letters a, b, c; and finally numbers and letters in parentheses. Thus, if you list I, you should list II (and perhaps III and IV and so on); if A, then B; if 1, then 2.

The roman numerals indicate the outline's main ideas. Indented capital letters provide main divisions within each main idea. The letters and numbers that follow list the supporting details and examples. Note the indentation of each subtopic. Any category can be expanded to fit the number of supporting details or examples that you wish to cover in the paper. Any lapses in logic are bound to surface if you use this system of organization, so you can catch and correct them before proceeding.

For example, look at the following abbreviated outline; item B is clearly a conspicuous lapse in logic:

   II. Gardner's theory of "intelligences"
     A. His definition of intelligence
     B. How did the concept of *g* originate?
     C. Seven kinds of intelligence

Item B should be moved from this section of the outline to the one pertaining to the *g*-centric view of intelligence. Some items may require a return to the library or the computer to clarify a point or to supplement parts of the outline with additional reference material.

Template for Writing and Note Taking

The outline is a way not only to organize your thoughts but also to make it easier to start writing. If you use the phrase or sentence format, the paper will almost write itself, as we see clearly in the following outline fragment:

II. Gardner's theory of "intelligences"
    A. Definition of intelligence
        1. ". . . the ability to solve problems, or to create products that are valued within one or more cultural settings" (Gardner, 1983, p. x)
        2. Criteria for intellectual talent (Gardner, 1983)
            a. Possible identification of intelligences by damage to particular areas of the brain
            b. Existence of exceptional populations (savants), implying the distinctive existence of a special entity

Had our hypothetical outline used complete sentences, the paper would write itself:

II. Gardner's theory of "intelligences"
    A. Definition of intelligence
        1. Gardner (1983) conceived of intelligence as "the ability to solve problems, or to create products that are valued within one or more cultural settings" (p. x).
        2. Gardner (1983) argued that a talent must fit eight criteria to be considered "intelligence."
            a. There is potential to isolate the intelligence by brain damage.
            b. Exceptional populations (e.g., savants) provide evidence of distinct entities.

In Chapter Two, we alluded to one other helpful hint about preparing an outline: You can use the outline's coding system to bring order to the notes you take during your literature search. If your notes refer to section "II.B.1" of your outline, you would write this code on the card, photocopy, or computer printout. Then, if you are using cards, for example, you can spread them on a large table and organize them by code.

Keep in mind, however, that the outline is only a guide. Its specific structure may change as you integrate your notes.

Outlining After the Fact

Some students write their papers over more than one semester (a senior thesis, for example) and may feel they cannot outline from the outset because they do not know where the final paper will go. When they do sit down to write, they tend to incorporate material from their earlier drafts, but they do not make an outline first. Still other students find the process of making an outline too exacting, preferring instead to sit at a word processor and let the stream of ideas flow spontaneously.

If either case describes you, then be sure to outline after the fact. To assure yourself that your work has an appealing, coherent form—what psychologists call a "good Gestalt"—make a "mini-table-of-contents" of your final draft, and then do a more detailed outline within the headings and subheadings. Ask yourself:

- Is the discussion focused, and do the ideas flow from or build on one another?
- Is there ample development of each idea?
- Are there supporting details for each main idea discussed?
- Are the ideas balanced?
- Is the writing to the point, or have I gone off on a tangent?

An experienced writer working with a familiar topic might be able to achieve success without a detailed outline. But for others, the lack of an outline often creates havoc and frustration, not to mention wasted time and effort. If you would like to practice on someone else's work, try outlining some section of John's. Ask yourself how well his discussion addresses the five preceding questions. If you find problems with the structure of his discussion, think of ways he could have avoided them or corrected them before submitting the final draft.

6

COMMUNICATING
STATISTICAL INFORMATION

Whether citing someone else's quantitative results in a review paper or describing your own detailed statistical analysis in a research report, the information should be presented clearly, accurately, precisely, and in enough detail to allow readers to reach their own conclusions. (If you will not be presenting any statistical information, you can skip this chapter and go on to Chapter Seven.)

Four Guidelines: CAPE

This chapter is for students who have taken an introductory course in statistics, or who are currently taking one and need to report statistical results in a literature review or a research report. In his review paper, John Smith quotes a researcher's statement that "approximately three fourths of the variance in real-world performance is not accounted for by intelligence test performance." But John properly cautions that "a predictor variable that can account for 25% of the variance is not unimpressive in the human sciences," and he cites an article buttressing this assertion. Some literature reviews, called *meta-analyses* (literally meaning the "analysis of analyses"), consist primarily of the use of statistical and graphical methods to summarize a group of similar studies. If you are preparing a research report, then you know that detailed statistical analyses are considered an essential part of the results section, as Jane Doe's report illustrates. (To jog your memory of standard statistical terms, Exhibit 14 lists some of the most common ones and their definitions.)

Although the information presented by Jane is the kind that is supposed to be routinely reported in journal articles, not every researcher provides all these details. For example, not always reported are effect sizes, although the APA publication manual reminds authors that, because the probability value does not directly reflect the magnitude of an effect or the strength of a relationship,

EXHIBIT 14 *Common statistical abbreviations and symbols*

Symbol/ Abbreviation	Definition
English symbols/Abbreviations	
ANOVA	Acronym for *analysis of variance,* a statistical procedure in which the total variance of a set of scores is partitioned into its components and *F* tests are used to statistically evaluate the difference between two or more means or variances.
CI	Confidence interval (i.e., the upper and lower bounds of a statistic); the confidence level is defined as $1 - \alpha$ (i.e., the probability that the range of values will contain the population value of the statistic).
d	Cohen's effect size index for the difference between two independent means, a descriptive statistic calibrated in standard score (*z*-score) units ranging from zero to positive or negative infinity.
df	Degrees of freedom.
F	Fisher's test of significance in ANOVA, used to evaluate the tenability of the null hypothesis of no difference between two or more means or variances.
g	Typically, Hedges's effect size index for the difference between two independent means, an inferential statistic calibrated in standard score (*z*-score) units ranging from zero to positive or negative infinity. (However, *g* is also used as a symbol for some other indices, including Cohen's *g* for the raw difference between a proportion and .50 and Cochran's *g* for comparing variabilities.)
M	The simple arithmetic average of a set of scores (i.e., the arithmetic mean).
Mdn	The median, or midmost score of a distribution.
MS	The unbiased estimate of the population variance, also symbolized as S^2.
n	The number of scores in one condition or subgroup of a study.
N	The total number of scores in a study.
p level	The probability of rejecting the null hypothesis when it is true (i.e., the probability of a Type I error).

"it is almost always necessary to include some index of effect size or strength of relationship in your Results section." We will have more to say about the distinction between the probability value and the effect size, but fortunately, as meta-analysts have discovered, there are ways of ferreting out effect sizes (and other missing statistical details) from the barest available ingredients. This chapter emphasizes four general guidelines for reporting statistical information, designated by the acronym CAPE, which stands for *c*larity, *a*ccuracy, *p*recision, and *e*nough detail to enable readers to make their own inferences. At the conclusion of the chapter, there is a list of annotated readings, including

EXHIBIT 14   Continued

Symbol/ Abbreviation	Definition
r	Pearson product-moment correlation, an index of the linear relationship between a pair of variables.
SD	Standard deviation, an index of the variability of a set of data around the mean value in a sample.
SS	The sum of the squared deviations from the mean in a set of scores.
t	A test of significance used to judge the tenability of the null hypothesis of no relationship between two variables (also called Student's t).
z score	Score converted to a standard deviation unit.

Greek symbols/Abbreviations

α	Alpha, the probability of a Type I error (i.e., the error of rejecting the null hypothesis when it is true), where $1 - \alpha$ is the confidence level. (The term *alpha* is also used to describe a measure of internal consistency reliability, known as *Cronbach's alpha*.)
β	Beta, the probability of a Type II error (i.e., the error of failing to reject the null hypothesis when it is false), where $1 - \beta$ (the probability of not making a Type II error) refers to the power of a statistical test.
λ	Lambda, a value in a set of coefficients (λ weights) that sum to zero and are used to state a prediction (illustrated in Jane Doe's research report in Appendix A).
σ	The standard deviation of a population of scores.
σ^2	The variance of a population of scores.
Σ	Instruction telling us to sum (add) a set of scores.
ϕ	Phi coefficient, the Pearson r where both variables are dichotomous.
χ^2	Chi-square, a statistic used to test the degree of agreement between the frequency data obtained and the frequency data expected under a particular hypothesis (e.g., the null hypothesis).

some "how-to" articles that illustrate particular data-analytic procedures and provide guidance on their use.

Reporting Results Clearly

Clarity of reporting means not obfuscating details in obscure or murky visual displays, or using technical terms inappropriately because you do not fully understand them, or reporting a diffuse analysis although you hypothesized a specific result (but never actually evaluated it statistically). Check with the instructor to get expert feedback on graphics, technical terms, and statistical analyses you want to use. (We will have more to say about diffuse statistical tests later on in this discussion.) It is also extremely important that the structure of your paper enable the reader to easily follow the logic of your reasoning. Writing the proposal (Chapter Three) was your initial attempt to develop a coherent structure. If you are writing a research report, the traditional structure in Chapter Four is designed to impose coherence on the presentation. If you are writing a review paper, the guidelines in Chapter Five should help you develop a coherent outline before you begin writing the first draft.

With the advent of computer graphics, it is easy to be lulled into a false sense of security about the clarity and interpretability of line graphs, bar graphs, pie charts, shaded maps, and so on. The APA manual advises the use of figures when you want to "convey at a quick glance an overall pattern of results," on the assumption that the figure actually communicates details more efficiently than words. Whether you are using figures or tables (as in Jane's report), you need to mention and interpret them in your text. If you are using figures, the APA manual's criteria for creating good figures are simplicity, clarity, and continuity. These are some additional guidelines:

◆ Use the figure to enhance what you say in the narrative text—that is, by supplementing or expanding on it.
◆ Don't encumber a figure with superfluous data or distracting details; it should be economical, communicating only essential facts.
◆ Use font, lines, labels, and symbols that are large enough, and easy enough to see, so the figure can be read easily.
◆ Use the same lettering in all figures, so the reader is not put off by different styles.
◆ The data should be precisely plotted. If you are drawing a figure by hand, use graph paper to keep the rows and columns evenly spaced, and then reduce the figure and paste it into your report.
◆ When graphing the relationship between an independent and a dependent variable (or between a predictor variable and a criterion or outcome variable), it is customary to put the independent (or predictor) variable on the horizontal axis (called the x axis, or the abscissa) and the dependent (or criterion) variable on the vertical axis (the y axis, or ordinate).
◆ The units should progress from small to large.

In his book *Elements of Graph Design,* Harvard cognitive psychologist Stephen M. Kosslyn wrote on how the brain perceives and processes visual information and what the implications are for visual displays (Kosslyn's book is listed in the annotated bibliography at the end of the chapter). As an illustration, because of how the brain developed, we are rarely aware of complex spatial relations between parts of a display, he concluded. Thus, it is frequently better to report complex data in a table, particularly if you want to communicate exact relations. Of course, another good reason for tables is that exact values can be provided, but when the data are summarized in figures, readers can make only an educated guess about the exact values.

If you plan to use color, Kosslyn offered the following tips:

- Choose colors that are well separated in the spectrum, because those close together are harder to discriminate. The colors perceived as being most separated are reddish purple, blue, yellowish gray, yellowish green, red, and bluish gray.
- Colors that, according to popular wisdom, are never confused (unless the person is color-blind) are white, gray, black, red, green, yellow, blue, pink, brown, orange, and purple. Use only a few of these colors, however, because using a lot of colors in the same visual display can confuse the reader.
- Avoid juxtaposing red (which has a relatively long wavelength) and blue (which has a relatively short wavelength), as they will be perceived as shimmering.
- Avoid cobalt blue, which is actually a mixture of blue and red and is hard to keep in focus. As an example, you may recall seeing a halo around blue streetlights at night, which you thought was due to fog; it was actually a visual phenomenon caused by your eyes' inability to focus the image properly.

Kosslyn summed up the psychological basis of graph design in three principles. The first is that "the mind is not a camera." That is, we do not see things only as they are because of the baggage we bring to every situation, such as experiential factors and expectancies. You remember the old proverb that "seeing is believing," but it is also true that believing is seeing, in that people tend to perceive in ways that fit into their expectations. A second principle is that "the mind judges a book by its cover," which means that people take appearance as a clue to reality. As an extreme example, imagine a figure that reports the results of two teams, called the Blue Team and the Red Team, but the graph uses blue ink to represent the Red Team and red ink to represent the Blue Team. This figure will inevitably create confusion, because the mind gravitates to physical appearance—in this case, to the color of the ink to infer the meaning of the words written in it. A third principle is that "the spirit is willing, but the mind is weak," which means that the visual and memory systems have natural limitations, which must be respected if visual displays are to be interpreted correctly.

Reporting Results Accurately

This second guideline requires the candid reporting of statistical results, not bending the facts by omitting relevant details or painting a picture that is slightly different from what was observed. Accuracy also means making a conscientious effort to avoid mistakes in recording and calculation—that is, checking all the different measurements, calculations, and numbers. Checking the raw data is a way to spot statistical outliers, which is the name for scores that lie far outside the normal range. Should you identify any, make sure they are not recording mistakes. Once you feel confident that the scores are recorded accurately, you may decide to report not only means but also medians as insurance against misleading interpretations. For example, suppose you wanted to describe the average income of a group of 10 people, and 9 of them were clustered together but the remaining person was far out on the scale. The median is not affected by the intrusion of this person's far-out income. Of course, it is prudent to report the range of incomes as well, so that readers are not misled into inferring that all 10 people were clustered together.

Accuracy also means being candid about when you formulated your hypotheses and predictions and not pretending that an ad hoc hypothesis (a conjecture developed on the spot after you inspected the data) was conceived before you saw the data. There is an old Bohemian legend about a fabled archer, known throughout the land, who was offered an empire by the king if he could teach him to be a great marksman. One day, the king came upon the archer standing next to a grove of trees. Each tree had a chalked circle and an arrow in the exact center of the circle; one arrow quivered in its circle even as the king approached. "Keep your empire," the honest archer told the king, "for the secret of my skill is that I shoot first and draw the circle afterward." Similarly, accuracy and honesty require that you inform readers which came first, the data or your hypothesis, because very little skill is required to come up with a "prediction" *after* you have inspected the data.

Accuracy and clarity frequently seem to be confounded, because the accurate reporting of information means describing a study in a way that is transparent rather than vague, including its design, conduct, analysis, and interpretation. As a case in point, randomized clinical trials (RCTs) in medical research have been criticized as being vague in the reporting of vital details about how the participants were allocated to groups or conditions. Despite educational efforts to correct this problem, it was noted recently that many medical studies report this information in an ambiguous way, which could result in biased estimates of the effectiveness of the clinical treatments.[1]

This case is also a reminder that inaccuracy is wasteful of resources and can be demoralizing, because biased conclusions and the misleading recommendations that result may lead to wasteful spending and false hopes. You may be wondering, however, what all this has to do with your research, as you are not conducting a clinical trial. The answer is that whatever the nature

---

[1] D. Moher, K. R. Schulz, & D. G. Altman. (2001). The CONSORT statement: Revised recommendations for improving the quality of reports of parallel-group randomized trials. *Annals of Internal Medicine, 134,* 657–662.

of the study, it is essential to describe the design, its implementation, the data analysis, and the interpretation as fully and accurately as possible.

There is another way in which inaccuracy is wasteful of resources, and it is a common problem. It concerns what might be described as "missing the forest for the p," because it pertains to how p values can cloud students' perceptions. We will have more to say about p values again in this chapter, but the point is not to behave as if there were some special place in the instructor's heart for students with p values less than .05, or to think that a nonsignificant p is evidence that the null hypothesis is true or that the effect size is zero. Your teacher will have just as much admiration for a "statistically nonsignificant" as for a "statistically significant" result, as long as the data are reported accurately and honestly, and appropriate implications are drawn. To help you avoid what University of Alberta experimental psychologist Peter Dixon has called the "p-value fallacy" of mistaking nonsignificant p values for evidence that the null hypothesis is true (Dixon's article appears in the list of annotated readings), here are some statistical guidelines if you are reporting t, F, or χ^2 tests:

◆ The expected value of a t test is 0 when the null hypothesis (H_0) is true.

◆ The expected value of F is usually a little above 1 when H_0 is true but can be accurately estimated by $df/(df - 2)$, where df refers to the denominator degrees of freedom. For Jane's $F(3,76) = 15.51$ (in Table 2), the expected value is $76/74 = 1.03$ when H_0 is true.

◆ The expected value of χ^2 is equal to the degrees of freedom when H_0 is true, so it would be 1 for a 2×2 chi-square, or 2 for a 2×3 chi-square, etc.

Reporting Results Precisely

Diffuse and precise significance tests are also referred to as omnibus and focused tests, respectively. An easy way to distinguish between them is to remember that all t tests, F tests with 1 degree of freedom in the numerator, and chi-square tests with 1 degree of freedom are focused significance tests, whereas all F tests with more than 1 degree of freedom in the numerator and all χ^2 tests with more than 1 degree of freedom are omnibus significance tests. Focused tests not only are more precise but usually are more powerful than omnibus significance tests; this is why focused significance tests are recommended for evaluating exact experimental predictions. We presume, of course, that your significance test is specifically addressed to your working hypothesis. If you used the wrong significance test or failed to pay heed to statistical power considerations, you might end up letting go of your working hypothesis prematurely, perhaps without even realizing it. If you know the old Tarzan movies, where he swings from tree to tree, you may also know that Tarzan was originally played by Johnny Weissmuller. When he was asked about his philosophy of life, Weissmuller's response was that "the main thing is not to let go of the vine." This is good advice for researchers as well: Know what you predicted, and hang onto it long enough to test your working hypotheses.

Finally, in reporting results precisely and candidly, try to strike a balance between being discursive and being falsely or needlessly precise. False precision means that something that is inherently vague is reported in overly exact terms. Suppose you used a standard attitude questionnaire in your research, and the participants responded on a 5-point scale from "strongly agree" to "strongly disagree." It would be false precision to report the means to a high number of decimal places, because your measuring instrument was not that sensitive to slight variations in attitudes. Needless precision means reporting the results more exactly than the circumstances require. Suppose you were reporting the weight of mouse subjects to six decimal places. Although your measuring instrument might be capable of this precision, the situation would not call for such exactitude. When in doubt, ask the instructor for guidance.

Reporting Enough Information

Earlier in this chapter, we mentioned the APA manual's recommendation "to include some index of effect size or strength of relationship in your Results section." *Effect size* is actually a general term that may, for example, refer to the difference in outcomes in two groups, or to the magnitude of the relationship between membership in these groups and scores on the dependent variable, or to a ratio of the odds of obtaining a particular outcome depending on the treatment condition. There are subtleties and nuances in the use of these and other effect size indicators (there are discussions in the annotated readings). The principal point, however, is that there are many ways of conceptualizing the effect size. One common effect size indicator in psychology is the Pearson product-moment correlation (r), which is used to indicate the strength of association between a predictor variable and a dependent variable, with $r_{effect\ size} = 1$ indicating a perfect linear relationship, and $r_{effect\ size} = 0$ indicating that neither variable can be predicted from the other by use of a linear equation. Another common effect size statistic is Cohen's d; it indicates the standardized difference between two group means (resembling a z score), with values ranging from zero to positive or negative infinity. Cohen's d of 0 would imply that normal distributions of the populations underlying the two groups are perfectly superimposed on one another, and $d = .8$ (Cohen called this a "large effect") would imply that the amount of nonoverlap is 47.4%.

There are good reasons to report the effect size, not just the p value of your significance test. One reason is that the p value depends a lot on the size of the sample, and therefore it is quite possible for the same magnitude of effect to be "significant" or "nonsignificant" depending on the number of sampling units (e.g., subjects) in your study. For example, the following table lists correlations (think of them as effect size *r*s) significant at $p = .05$ (two-tailed):

$N - 2$	r
1	.997
2	.950
3	.878
4	.811
5	.754
10	.576
20	.423
30	.349
40	.304
50	.273
100	.195
200	.138
300	.113
500	.088
1,000	.062
2,000	.044

The first column of numbers, labeled "$N - 2$," refers to the total sample size minus 2, which is the definition of the degrees of freedom (*df*) for a correlation; the second column shows the magnitude of the *r* required to be significant at $p = .05$ two-tailed. This table shows that an effect size *r* can be statistically significant no matter whether it is a very large effect or a very small effect. What counts most in the table is that the total sample size was sufficiently large to enable the *r* in question to be detected at the desired level of significance (in this case, $p = .05$ two-tailed). Notice that an effect size as small as $r = .044$ is significant at $p = .05$ with a total sample (*N*) of 2,002, but an *r* thirteen times larger is not statistically significant at the same *p* level with a total sample of 12. You can see why reporting only a *p* value would not give the reader a clue as to the magnitude of the effect.

Another way of thinking about significance testing and effect size is summarized by the following conceptual equation:

$$\text{significance test} = \text{effect size} \times \text{study size}$$

which simply explains that significance tests (e.g., *t*, *F*, or χ^2) can be understood as comprising two components, one of which is a reflection of the magnitude of the effect (e.g., *r* or Cohen's *d*), and the other, the number of participants or sampling units in the study (i.e., the study size). You know that the larger the value of the significance test (i.e., the bigger the *t*, *F*, or χ^2), the smaller (and usually more coveted) is the *p* value.

For example, one way to describe a t test in the style of the conceptual equation above is

$$t = d \times \frac{\sqrt{df}}{2}$$

where df = the total sample size minus 2, and the effect size indicator is Cohen's d, which can be estimated by

$$d = \frac{M_1 - M_2}{\sigma_{pooled}}$$

where the difference between two group means (M_1 and M_2) is divided by the pooled population standard deviation. The implication is that the value of t will increase as the difference between means M_1 and M_2 increases, as variability within the groups (i.e., the σ_{pooled}) decreases, and the total sample size increases. If you were designing an experiment, you could try to maximize your significance test by (a) selecting the strongest manipulation that was ethically and practically feasible, thus driving the means further apart; (b) choosing a homogeneous sample of subjects and a standardized procedure, thus minimizing the variability within groups; and/or (c) recruiting as many subjects as you can afford or as are practical to run, thus increasing the study size.

As we said, the product-moment r and Cohen's d are not the only effect size indicators that are used in research in psychology. Furthermore, the product-moment r comes in different forms. For example, the point-biserial correlation (r_{pb}) is a Pearson r that indexes the strength of association between a dichotomous variable (*biserial* implies two sets of measures, such as female gender vs. male gender, or control group vs. experimental group) and a continuous variable (*point* means a value on a continuum). The phi coefficient (ϕ) is a Pearson r that is used to measure the degree of association between two dichotomous variables. In the appendix section of Jane's report, she notes that she computed another effect size correlation, $r_{alerting}$, which takes its name from the fact that squaring it (i.e., $r^2_{alerting}$) "alerted" her to the proportion of the between-conditions sum of squares that could be accounted for by her linear contrast weights. Because there are different effect size indices, and thus different ranges, you always need to state which effect size measure you used.

The APA manual also advises that researchers try to report confidence intervals for population estimates such as means, proportions, and effect sizes. The confidence interval gives the upper and lower estimated bounds of the statistic, and the confidence level (defined as $1 - \alpha$) indicates how "approximate" the estimated population statistic is. Thus, 95% confidence implies that there are 95 chances in 100 that the population value (e.g., a mean, a proportion, or an effect size) falls within the specified confidence interval. If you increased the level of confidence—say, from 95% to 99%—you would widen the interval. Similarly, reducing the level of confidence from 95% to 90% would shrink the confidence interval. To understand why this is so, think of how wide an interval you would need to be 100% sure about some risky event.

Before we leave this discussion of "how much information is enough," the following checklist will serve as a reminder of the statistical information recommended in the APA manual:

- ◆ Report the values of your test statistics (e.g., t, F, χ^2), their degrees of freedom (df), and the probability (p) of obtaining values as extreme as or more extreme than the value of each test statistic.
- ◆ Particularly in the case of t tests (and z tests), it is also important to indicate whether the p value is directional (one-tailed) or nondirectional (two-tailed).
- ◆ Report the effect sizes of all focused tests (i.e., t tests, F tests with numerator $df = 1$, and one-df χ^2 tests), and interpret the effect sizes in the context of your study and of the variables you are measuring.
- ◆ Report the confidence intervals of estimated population means, proportions, and effect sizes, and interpret all the results accordingly.
- ◆ Report sample sizes and measures of variability.
- ◆ Pay heed to statistical power, particularly if you are reporting a significance test that was not statistically significant (see Jane's discussion section for an illustration).

Pentimento

If you are writing a review paper, then you know that not all the information above is routinely reported in journal articles. However, as mentioned earlier, even when statistical information is missing, there may be a way of simulating or re-creating it from the barest of ingredients. For example, one of the recommended readings below describes how to estimate effect sizes in experimental studies from just the reported sample sizes and a precise p value (see Rosenthal and Rubin's $r_{equivalent}$ statistic). The novelist Lillian Hellman wrote a book entitled *Pentimento,* a term borrowed from art restoration, that refers to a hidden image, usually one that has been painted over. As paintings age, the old paint tends to become transparent, and sometimes almost translucent, and we may begin to perceive something beneath the surface. Similarly, for students skilled enough in statistical reasoning and enterprising enough to want to explore the data further, there is useful information waiting to be restored beneath the surface of research reports. Further discussion of this topic is beyond the scope of this book, but we mention it to whet your curiosity and interest, because it can be as much fun as solving a good mystery story.

Annotated Readings

To learn more about the topics discussed in this chapter, the most readily accessible source is your statistics or research methods text and its Web page links. Encyclopedias in psychology and related areas are often a source of general information, such as A. E. Kazdin's *Encyclopedia of Psychology*

(Oxford University Press & American Psychological Association, 2000), N. J. Smelser and P. B. Baltes's *International Encyclopedia of the Social and Behavioral Sciences* (Elsevier, 2002), and M. Lewis-Beck, A. E. Bryman, and T. F. Liao's *Sage Encyclopedia of Social Science Methods* (Sage, 2004). The readings listed below were generally selected on the basis of their accessibility to students. Articles with how-to instructions and illustrations are denoted by an asterisk (*), and numbers printed before readings indicate a suggested sequence in which they should be read:

Significance Testing and Statistical Power

1. Cohen, J. (1990). Things I have learned (so far). *American Psychologist, 45,* 1304–1312. Classic article, in which the late Jacob Cohen discusses the role of statistical power in null hypothesis significance testing (NHST) and laments the fact that so many researchers who engage in NHST pay no attention to power and, as a consequence, frequently end up handicapping themselves without even realizing it.

*2. Cohen, J. (1992). A power primer. *Psychological Bulletin, 112,* 155–159. Discussion and summary table of sample sizes needed to detect "small," "medium," and "large" effects at alpha = .01, .05, and .10 for the most common statistical tests used in psychological research.

3. Hallahan, M., & Rosenthal, R. (1996). Statistical power: Concepts, procedures, and applications. *Behaviour Research and Therapy, 34,* 489–499. Overall tutorial discussion of statistical power and its applications to psychological research, including 10 procedures for increasing power.

4. Dixon, P. (2003). The *p*-value fallacy and how to avoid it. *Canadian Journal of Experimental Psychology, 57,* 189–202. Discussion of misusing significance tests to decide whether an effect is absent or present, such as misconstruing the failure to reject the null hypothesis as evidence that the effect in question is zero or negligible.

Effect Size Indicators

*1. Rosnow, R. L., & Rosenthal, R. (2003). Effect sizes for experimenting psychologists. *Canadian Journal of Experimental Psychology, 57,* 221–237. Describes three families of effect size indicators in a variety of cases, and the interpretation as well as the limitations of particular effect size indices such as the odds ratio, relative risk, and risk difference in clinical trials.

*2. Rosenthal, R., & Rubin, B. (2003). $r_{equivalent}$: A simple effect size estimator. *Psychological Methods, 8,* 492–496. Describes how to ferret out a point-biserial effect size r or a Cohen's d from just the sample size, N, and a p value, a procedure that can also be used when reporting nonparametric statistics for which effect size indices have not been developed.

*3. Rosnow, R. L., Rosenthal, R., & Rubin, D. B. (2000). Contrasts and correlations in effect-size estimation. *Psychological Science, 11,* 446–453. Formulas for calculating *r,* Cohen's *d,* and Hedges's *g* from independent *t* tests, and for converting Hedges's *g* into *r;* also included is a formula for estimating the loss of power in unequal-*n* designs relative to equal-*n* designs. Effect size correlations for use with focused tests on more than two independent groups are also discussed.

Confidence and Null-Counternull Intervals

Fidler, F., Thomason, N., Cumming, G., Finch, S., & Leeman, J. (2004). Editors can lead researchers to confidence intervals, but can't make them think: Statistical reform lessons from medicine. *Psychological Science, 15,* 119–126. Although confidence intervals have for years been routinely reported in medical journals and are also recommended in the APA publication manual, they have yet to become standard in psychology. This article reiterates the useful role of confidence intervals.

*Masson, E. J., & Loftus, G. R. (2003). Using confidence intervals for graphically based data interpretations. *Canadian Journal of Experimental Psychology, 57,* 203–220. Illustrates the use of confidence intervals in figures and graphs.

*Rosenthal, R., & Rubin, D. B. (1994). The counternull value of an effect size: A new statistic. *Psychological Science, 5,* 329–334. The counternull statistic, which is conceptually related to confidence intervals, involves the obtained effect size and the null hypothesis and is insurance against prematurely believing the null hypothesis to be true when the *p* value is greater than .05.

Meta-analysis and Focused Statistical Tests

Rosenthal, R., & DiMatteo, M. R. (2001). Meta-analysis: Recent developments in quantitative methods for literature reviews. *Annual Review of Psychology, 52,* 59–82. Introduction to meta-analysis, which also addresses basic questions concerning its use to summarize related studies and to identify variables that moderate observed relationships.

*Rosnow, R. L., & Rosenthal, R. (1996). Computing contrasts, effect sizes, and counternulls on other people's published data: General procedures for research consumers. *Psychological Methods, 1,* 331–340. Statistical procedures for computing focused *t, F,* and *z* tests on more than two independent groups, as well as their interpretation by Cohen's d, Hedges's g, and the Pearson r and the construction of confidence limits and the null-counternull interval.

Figures, Graphs, and Other Visual Displays

The following are three useful reference texts for the presentation of graphical information, whether you are writing a paper for a course assignment or have left the academic ivory tower and entered the world of business or government:

Kosslyn, S. M. (1994). *Elements of graph design*. New York: W. H. Freeman.

Tufte, E. R. (2001). *The visual display of quantitative information* (2nd ed.). Cheshire, CT: Graphics Press.

Wainer, H. (1997). *Visual revelations: Graphical tales of fate and deception from Napoleon Bonaparte to Ross Perot*. Mahwah, NJ: Erlbaum.

7

WRITING AND POLISHING

Writing a first draft is a little like taking the first dip in chilly ocean waters on a hot day. It may be uncomfortable at the outset but feels better once you get used to it. In this chapter, we provide some pointers to buoy you up as you begin writing.

Sorting Through Your Material

Back in 1947, there was a fascinating story in newspapers and magazines about two brothers, the Collyers, who were found dead in a rubbish-filled mansion at Fifth Avenue and 128th Street in New York City. On receiving a tip that one brother, Homer Collyer, had died, the police forced their way into the mansion with crowbars and axes. They found all of the entrances to the house blocked by wrapped packages of newspapers, hundreds of cartons, and all kinds of junk (14 grand pianos, most of a Model T Ford, the top of a horse-drawn carriage, a tree limb 7 feet long and 20 inches in diameter, an organ, a trombone, a cornet, three bugles, five violins, three World War I bayonets, and 10 clocks, including one 9 feet high and weighing 210 pounds). The rooms and hallways were honeycombed with tunnels through all this debris and booby-trapped so that anything disturbed would come crashing down on an intruder. The police began searching for the other brother, Langley, who had been caring for Homer, as it was thought that he might have phoned in the tip. After 8 weeks of burrowing through the incredible mess, they finally found the body of Langley Collyer wedged between a chest of drawers and a bedspring; he had been killed by one of his own booby traps.

For students writing literature reviews and research reports, the lesson of the Collyer brothers is that it is not always easy to discard things you have made an effort to save, including notes, studies, and quotes that you have taken the trouble to track down. But quantity cannot replace quality and relevance in the material you save for your paper. Instructors are more impressed by tightly reasoned papers than by ones that are overflowing with superfluous material. It is best to approach the writing and polishing stage with an open but focused mind—that is, a mind that is focused on the objective but that is at the same time open to discarding irrelevant material (not research data, however).

The Self-Motivator Statement

To begin the first draft, write down somewhere for yourself the purpose or goal you have in mind (that is, what your paper will be about). Keep this "self-motivator statement" brief so that you have a succinct focus for your thoughts as you enter them into your word processor or set them down on paper. On the assumption that you consulted your instructor and afterward jotted down the ideas you spoke about, you can draw on these notes to help you write your self-motivator statement.

If we refer to the two sample papers at the end of this book, we can imagine the following self-motivators after the students had consulted with their instructors, thought about their notes, and formulated an overall plan:

From John Smith

I'm going to compare the *g*-centered view of intelligence with what I am going to term the *multiplex view* because the way that different abilities are subsumed under the term *intelligence* reminds me of how different movies are housed together in a multiplex theater. I will emphasize Howard Gardner's theoretical approach, the criticisms, and the counter-arguments. At the end, I will try to say something about both current and future directions of research on intelligence.

From Jane Doe

I'm going to describe how I found that tipping increases when people are given a small gift, and how the manipulation of a reciprocity effect can further increase tipping. I will begin with a background review that puts my hypotheses in context, and I will conclude with some observations and ideas for further research.

As you can see, this trick of using a self-motivator statement can help to concentrate your thoughts. It should also make the task of writing seem less formidable. The self-motivator is a good way simply to get you going and keep you clearheaded, and it is also a good way to filter out material that can be discarded. You will be less apt to go off on a tangent if every once in a while you glance at this statement to remind yourself of your plan for the paper's direction.

The Opening

A good opening is crucial if the reader's attention and interest are to be engaged. Some writers are masters at creating good openings, but many technical articles and books in psychology start out ponderously. There are certainly enough cases of ponderous writing so that we need not give examples. But what about openings that grip our minds and make us want to delve further into the work?

One technique for beginning a paper in an inviting way is to pose a stimulating question. For example, psychologist Sissela Bok wrote a book about the ethics of lying, ostensibly a pretty dry and uninviting subject to many people, but she opened her book (*Lying: Moral Choice in Public and Private Life*, Pantheon, 1978) with a number of compelling questions that resonate with immediacy and vibrancy:

> Should physicians lie to dying patients so as to delay the fear and anxiety which the truth might bring them? Should professors exaggerate the excellence of their students on recommendations in order to give them a better chance in a tight job market? Should parents conceal from children the fact that they were adopted? Should social scientists send investigators masquerading as patients to physicians in order to learn about racial and sexual biases in diagnosis and treatment? Should government lawyers lie to Congressmen who might otherwise oppose a much-needed welfare bill? And should journalists lie to those from whom they seek information in order to expose corruption? (p. xv)

By posing these questions, the author speaks to readers in the same way that she would if she were opening a dialogue. If we think about the questions, even for a moment, we are compelled to answer them, even if only subconsciously. We are drawn into the book because we want to compare Bok's answers to her questions with our own thinking (what psychologist Leon Festinger described as "social comparison").

Another technique is to try to rivet attention by impressing on readers the paradoxical nature of a timely issue. In *Obedience to Authority* (Harper, 1969), social psychologist Stanley Milgram began as follows:

> Obedience is as basic an element in the structure of social life as one can point to. Some system of authority is a requirement of all communal living, and it is only the man dwelling in isolation who is not forced to respond, through defiance or submission, to the commands of others. Obedience, as a determinant of behavior, is of particular relevance to our time. It has been reliably established that from 1933 to 1945 millions of innocent people were systematically slaughtered on command. Gas chambers were built, death camps were guarded, daily quotas of corpses were produced with the same efficiency as the manufacture of appliances. These inhumane policies may have originated in the mind of a single person, but they could only have been carried out on a massive scale if a very large number of people obeyed orders. (p. 1)

Milgram's passage first stirs our imagination because it reminds us that obedience is a basic part of social life. What ultimately draws us into Milgram's book is the matter-of-fact way he refers to the grotesque nature of the Holocaust, letting the deadly facts speak for themselves. He leads us to a logical conclusion, setting the stage for the rest of his thesis. Incidentally, this passage was written before there were concerns about sexist language: Milgram's use of the word *man* ("it is only the man dwelling in isolation") as a general term for men and women is now considered improper usage. Instead, he could have said "the person dwelling in isolation" (we return to this issue later).

However, perhaps you are thinking, "What does Milgram's or Bok's work have to do with me? These are Ph.D. psychologists who were writing for publication, and I'm just writing a paper for a course." The answer any instructor will give you is that an expectation of good writing that captures the reader's attention and draws the reader into the message is not limited to published work. It also applies, for instance, to correspondence in businesses and organizations, company memos, and applications for jobs.

In the sample papers at the end of this book, what makes the opening passages inviting is that they also strike a resonant chord in the reader. There are many other useful opening techniques. A definition, an anecdote (for example, the strange case of the Collyer brothers), a metaphor that compares or contrasts (such as using *the Collyer brothers* as a synonym for pack rats), an opening quotation (called an *epigraph*), and so on—all of these are devices that a writer can use to shape a beginning paragraph. Not only should the opening lead the reader into the work, but it should also provide momentum for the writer as the words begin to flow. John Smith begins his review paper by implying a paradox, which is that we ordinarily speak of "intelligence" in many different ways, but psychologists have traditionally viewed it in one general way. Jane Doe's research report starts with interesting facts, which immediately lead into the logic of her introduction, and ultimately to her hypotheses.

Settling Down to Write

Should you find yourself still having trouble beginning the introductory section, try the trick of not starting with the introductory paragraph. Start writing whatever paragraph or section you feel will be the easiest, and then tackle the rest as your ideas begin to flow. When faced with a blank computer screen and a flashing cursor, some students escape by surfing the Net, playing video games, taking a nap, or wandering around to find somebody to chat with. Recognize these and similar counterproductive moves for what they are, because they can drain your energies. Use them instead as rewards *after* you have done a good job of writing.

The following are general pointers to ensure that your initial writing will go as smoothly as possible:

- While writing, try to work in a quiet, well-lighted place in 2-hour stretches (dim lighting makes people sleepy). Even if you are under time pressure to finish the paper quickly, it is important to take a break so you can collect your thoughts and make sure you are not writing aimlessly or drifting off in a wrong direction.
- When you take a break, go for a stroll, preferably outside, because the fresh air will be invigorating, and the change of environment will help you think about what you have already written and what you want to say next.
- If you are unexpectedly called away while you are in the middle of an idea, jot down a phrase or a few words that will get you back on track once you return to your writing. (Be sure to save your work before you leave.)
- When you stop for the day, try to stop at a point that is midway through a thought that you are finding difficult to express or complete. When you wake up the next day, your mind will be fresh with new ideas, and your writing will not have to start cold.
- Try to pace your work with time to spare so that you can complete the first draft and let it rest for a day. When you return to the completed first draft after a night's sleep, your critical powers will be enhanced, and you will have a fresh approach to shaping the final draft.

Ethics of Writing and Reporting

The most fundamental ethical principle in scholarly writing is honesty in all aspects of the work. If you are conducting empirical research and writing a report, this principle means honesty in all aspects of the project, from its implementation to your public account of the procedures that you used, your findings, their limitations, and their plausible implications. Two prime examples of deliberate dishonesty are the falsification of data and the fabrication of results, which constitute fraud. In the same way that the professional career of a researcher who falsifies data or fabricates results is compromised, the consequences will be harsh for the student writing a research report in which the data or results are fabricated.

Knowingly misrepresenting the implications of actual findings is also unethical, whether it involves what Robert Rosenthal has called *hyperclaiming* (i.e., exaggerating the implications of research) or *causism* (i.e., falsely implying a causal relationship). For example, using expressions such as "the effect of," "the impact of," "the consequence of," and "as a result of" clearly implies that there is a causal relationship. But if the research design does not allow you to make a causal inference, you are guilty of hyperclaiming by using this language. To avoid this problem, simply use the appropriate language, including expressions like "was related to," "was predictable from," or "could be inferred from." As Rosenthal has argued, if the writer is aware of the problem, then the causism reflects blatant unethical misrepresentation and deception; if the writer is unaware, then it reflects ignorance or lazy writing.

Honesty in research reporting and other scholarly writing also means giving credit where credit is due. For students, this means that if the instructor, a teaching assistant, or someone else helped you in some significant way, you acknowledge that contribution in your narrative or in a footnote. Should your research later become part of an article authored by your instructor, the decision as to whether you will be listed as a coauthor or in a footnote acknowledgment will depend on the nature of your contribution to the research. If the article is substantially based on your individual efforts (as in a dissertation or a senior thesis), you will usually be listed as a coauthor, possibly even as the principal author, depending on the extent of your contribution.

Another important ethical standard concerns the sharing of data with those who want to verify published claims by reanalyzing the results. Provided that the confidentiality of the study participants is protected, and unless legal rights preclude the release of the data, psychologists are expected to make their empirical findings available to other competent professionals. Instructors have the option to require students writing research reports to provide the raw data on which the work is based. If confidentiality is a potential problem, ask the instructor how the data might be coded to protect the privacy of those who have participated in your study.

Before we turn to what many instructors consider the most significant concern in student papers—the avoidance of plagiarism—we will mention one further standard with implications for students. It is unethical to misrepresent as fresh data any research results that have already been published or reported. If the data have already been published or reported elsewhere, the researcher is expected to say so and to tell where. The reason for this rule is to avoid leading research consumers to mistakenly believe that a separate report of the same research findings implies that the research has been successfully replicated. The implication for students is that it is unacceptable to submit the same work for additional credit in different courses. It may be acceptable to base the literature review in a research report for one course on the more extensive review in a paper for another course, but only with the full knowledge and consent of the instructors.

Avoiding Plagiarism

The most nagging concern of most instructors who teach writing-intensive courses is conveying the meaning and consequences of plagiarism. The term *plagiarism,* which comes from a Latin word meaning "kidnapper," refers to the theft of another person's ideas or work and passing it off as your own. It is crucial that you understand what constitutes plagiarism and be aware that the penalties can be severe. Claiming not to know that you committed plagiarism is not an acceptable defense. Simply stated, stealing someone else's work or paying for it on the Internet and passing it off as your own is wrong, and the penalty in a class assignment or a thesis will be severe.

In fact, it is easy to avoid committing plagiarism. All you must be is attentive and willing to make the effort to paraphrase the passage in question (and cite the source exactly), or else to quote the passage word for word and put quotation marks around it (and, of course, cite the source and page number). If the passage is lengthy (40 or more words), as illustrated by the two passages that we quoted previously from Bok's and Milgram's books, then quotation marks are not used; instead the passage is set off as a *block quotation* (indented about a half inch from the left margin, with the page number indicated in parentheses after the final period).

To illustrate plagiarism and how easily it can be avoided, assume that a student writing an essay came across Sissela Bok's book on lying and copied down the following passage for future reference:

> Deceit and violence—these are two forms of deliberate assault on human beings. Both can coerce people into acting against their will. Most harm that can befall victims through violence can come to them also through deceit. But deceit controls more subtly, for it works on belief as well as action. Even Othello, whom few would have dared to try to subdue by force, could be brought to destroy himself and Desdemona through falsehood. (Bok, 1978, p. 18)

There would be no problem if the student reproduced this passage just as it appears here, because the student has copied the passage accurately, clearly indicated that it is quoted from Bok's work (by indenting the entire passage), and has properly noted the page on which it appeared. The plagiarism problem would arise if the student decided to change a word or two to make the passage sound a little different and then passed it off as an original thought. No need to mention Bok's book, the student thinks, because no one will bother to check, and even if the instructor should happen to recognize this passage, why, the student can plead "forgetting" to give Bok full credit. The student submits a paper containing the following passage incorporated into the narrative text (that is, it is not indicated as a quote with a few words changed):

> Deceit and violence are two forms of deliberate assault on human beings. Both can coerce people into acting against their will. Most harm that can happen to people through violence can also happen to them through deceit. However, deceit controls more subtly, because it works on belief as well as action. Even Othello, whom few would have dared to try to subdue by force, could be brought to destroy himself and Desdemona through falsehood.

Although it might sound like an A paper to the student, the passage when seen in the context of the rest of the paper will stick out like a sore thumb, and instructors are sensitive to inconsistencies like these. When the student is caught, the result will be an F in the course. But even if not caught red-handed, the student must nevertheless live with the knowledge of this deceit and worry that the dishonesty may at some later point come back to haunt him or her.

Another word of caution: One instructor mentioned to us that, "although changing a word or two of an author's writing, failing to cite the source, and just passing it off as one's own work is certainly egregious, it is not the problem that many instructors run into more frequently." A more frequent problem, this instructor told us, is that students start off with something like "According to Bok (1978) . . ." and change some words, and simply repeat a passage without indicating that it is a word-for-word quote (or almost a word-for-word quote). Just changing a word or two in each sentence is not legal paraphrasing; it's plagiarism. The student needs to put the author's ideas into his or her own words, including his or her own sentence structure.

Of course, if you believe that someone else has said something much better than you ever hope to say it, quote (and cite) or paraphrase (and cite) the other source. For example, here is how the student might have incorporated Bok's ideas without falling into plagiarism:

> Bok (1978) made the case that deceit and violence "can coerce people into acting against their will" (p. 18). Deceit, she argued, controls more subtly because it affects belief. Using a literary analogy, Bok observed, "Even Othello, whom few would have dared to try to subdue by force, could be brought to destroy himself and Desdemona through falsehood" (p. 18).

Electronic plagiarizing is no more acceptable than plagiarizing from printed matter. If you find something on the Internet that you want to use, the same considerations of honesty apply. Some instructors have mentioned that they use a specialized search engine to randomly check their students' titles and phraseology for stolen material or uncredited citations. One instructor told us how he typed the title of a student's paper into a search engine and the entire paper came up on a Web site! With the growing accessibility of specialized search tools engineered to detect this problem, the likelihood of not getting caught is diminishing rapidly. As previously mentioned, it is a good idea to keep your notes, outlines, and rough drafts, because instructors will ask students for such material if a question arises about the originality of their work.

Lazy Writing

On hearing that quotations and citations are not construed by definition as plagiarism, some lazy students submit papers saturated with quoted material. Unless you feel it is absolutely essential, avoid quoting lengthy passages throughout a paper. What, then, would be appropriate occasions for quoting someone? One situation would be if you were describing two competing views and wanted to be sure to represent both positions fairly. Another situation is when someone's language is so expressive and convincing that you believe it would improve your presentation to quote a portion of it.

Thus, there are occasions when it may be advisable to quote something (with a citation, of course). However, quoting a statement that is not particularly momentous or poignant signals lazy writing. Your instructor expects your paper to reflect *your* thoughts after you have examined and synthesized material from sources you found pertinent. The penalty for lazy writing is not as severe as that for plagiarism, but it may mean a reduced grade in writing-intensive courses. The reason for a lowered grade is that lazy writing conveys the impression that the student has not put very much effort into the assignment. Furthermore, if you really cannot express an idea in your own words, your instructor will conclude that you do not understand it well enough to write about it.

Tone

As you write, there are certain basic style points to keep in mind. The *tone* of your paper is the manner and attitude that are reflected in the way you express your ideas. Your writing should not sound arrogant or pompous, nor should it be either dull or flowery. How can you create an appropriate tone in a scholarly essay or research report in psychology? The answer is that it takes a lot of practice, and in the process of becoming skilled, you can learn by paying attention to how successful researchers and scholars express their ideas in an appropriate tone.

Here are some tips on how to create the right tone:

♦ Strive for an explicit, straightforward, interesting, but not emotional way of expressing your thoughts, findings, and conclusions (as illustrated in the sample papers).

♦ Try not to sound stilted or uncomfortably formal (instead of saying, "In the opinion of this writer . . ." just state your opinion—period).

♦ Don't write in such a casual or informal way, however, that your paper reads like a letter to a favorite aunt ("Here's what Jones and Smith say . . ." or "So I told the research participants . . .").

♦ Try not to sound slick, like the glib reports on network TV and in supermarket tabloids.

♦ Strive for an objective, direct tone that keeps your reader subordinate to the material you are presenting. Instead of saying, "The reader will note that the results were . . . ," say, "The results were . . ."

♦ If your instructor finds it acceptable, don't be afraid to use the first person, but don't refer to yourself as *we* unless you are clearly referring to a collaborative effort with someone else.

♦ Avoid wordiness. A famous writing manual is *The Elements of Style* (Allyn & Bacon, 2000) by William Strunk, Jr., and E. B. White. One of Professor Strunk's admonitions is "Omit needless words. Omit needless words. Omit needless words."

Nonsexist Language

The question of *word gender* has become a matter of some sensitivity among many writers. One reason to discourage sex bias in written and spoken communication is that words can influence people's thoughts and deeds, and we do not want to reinforce stereotypes or prejudiced behaviors. However, there is sometimes a good reason not to use gender-free pronouns. Suppose a new drug has been tested only on male subjects. If the researchers used only gender-free pronouns when referring to their subjects, a reader might mistakenly infer that the results applied to both sexes.

The point, of course, is to think before you write. In her book *The Elements of Nonsexist Usage* (Prentice Hall, 1990), Val Dumond made the following observation concerning overuse of the word *man*: "When the word is used, that is the mental picture that is formed. The picture is what simultaneously represents a conceptual meaning to the interpreter. Since a female picture does not come to mind when the word *man* is used, it would follow that man does not represent in any way a female human" (p. 1).

When the issues of nonsexist language first gained prominence, writers used contrived words such as *s/he* and *he/she* to avoid sexist language. Not only are the forms *he/she* and *s/he* awkward, but if the actors in question are of one gender, the use of *he/she* or *s/he* would mislead the reader into thinking that the actors included both genders. Another contrived practice is using the plural pronoun *they* as a singular pronoun to avoid using *he* to represent both genders. An example: "When a *person* [singular] takes an idea from a published source, *they* [plural pronoun] must cite that source appropriately." Because the subject (the "person") is singular, it is grammatically incorrect to use the plural pronoun *they*. One acceptable alternative is to say she or he rather than they ("When a *person* takes an idea from a published source, *she or he* must cite that source appropriately"). A less wordy alternative is to make the entire sentence plural ("When *people* take ideas from published sources, *they* must cite those sources appropriately").

In general, beware of masculine nouns and pronouns that will give a sex bias to your writing. There are two simple rules:

◆ Use plural pronouns when you are referring to both genders—for instance, "They did . . ." instead of "He did . . ." and ". . . to them" instead of ". . . to him."
◆ Use masculine and feminine pronouns if the situation calls for them. For example, if the study you are discussing used only male subjects, the use of only masculine pronouns is appropriate.

Voice

The verb forms you use in your writing can speak with one of two voices: active or passive. You write in the *active voice* when you represent the subject of your sentence as performing the action expressed by your verb ("The study participant responded by . . ."). You write in the *passive voice* when the subject of your sentence undergoes the action expressed by your verb ("The response was made by the study participant . . .").

If you try to rely mainly on the active voice, you will have a more vital, compelling style:

Active Voice (Good)

Eleanor Gibson (1988) argued that perceptual development in humans is "an ever-spiraling path of discovery" (p. 37).

Passive Voice (Not as Good)

It was argued by Eleanor Gibson (1988) that perceptual development in humans is "an ever-spiraling path of discovery" (p. 37).

This quoted passage also illustrates when it is advisable to quote. The reason the student chose this fragment is that it is especially expressive and eloquent, whereas trying to paraphrase it might not capture Gibson's idea with the same flair. Furthermore, quoting such an eminent authority as Eleanor Gibson lends weight to the student's development of a particular argument.

Verb Tense

The verb tenses you use in your paper can get into a tangle unless you observe the following basic rules:

- Use the *past tense* to report studies that were done in the past ("Jones and Smith found . . ."). If you are writing a research report, both the method and results sections can usually be written in the past tense because your study has already been accomplished ("In this study, data *were* collected . . ." and "In these questionnaires, there *were* . . .").
- Use the *present tense* to define terms ("Multiplex, in this context, *means* . . ." and "A stereotype *is* defined as . . ."). The present tense is also frequently used to state a general hypothesis or to make a general claim ("Winter days *are* generally shorter than summer days").
- The *future tense* can be saved for the section of your paper in which you discuss implications for further investigation ("Future research *will be* necessary . . ."). But it is not essential to use the future tense. Instead, you could say, "Further investigation *is* warranted . . ."

Notice that three periods appear at the end of some of the examples in the above list. The name for these periods is an *ellipsis mark*, and its purpose in these examples is to indicate that the sentences continue. Although as a general rule the ellipsis is not used at the end of a quotation, we use it in these examples just to introduce you to this punctuation mark. Typically, the ellipsis is used somewhere in the middle of a lengthy quoted passage to indicate that selected words have been omitted.

Agreement of Subject and Verb

Make sure each sentence expresses a complete thought and has a *subject* (in general terms, something that performs the action) and a *verb* (an action that is performed or a state of being).

Subject and Verb Agree

The study participants [subject] were [verb] introductory psychology students who were fulfilling a course requirement.

Because the subject is plural (*study participants*), the verb form used (*were*) is also plural. Thus, the verb and subject agree, a basic rule of grammar. In most sentence forms, achieving this agreement is a simple matter. But trouble can sometimes arise, so here are some tips:

◆ When you use *collective nouns* (those that name a group), they can be either singular or plural—for example, *committee, team, faculty.* When you think of the group as a single unit, use a singular verb ("The union *is* ready to settle"). Plurals are called for when you want to refer to the components of a group ("The faculty *were* divided on the issue").

◆ Trouble can pop up when words come between subject and verb: "Therapy [singular subject], in combination with behavioral organic methods of weight gain, exemplifies [singular verb form] this approach." It would be incorrect to write, "Therapy, in combination with behavioral organic methods of weight gain, *exemplify* [plural verb form] this approach."

◆ Use a *singular verb form* after the following: *each, either, everyone, someone, neither, nobody.* Here is a correct usage: "When everyone is ready, the experiment will begin."

Common Usage Errors

Confusing Homonyms

Instructors see frequent usage errors in student papers. The inside front cover of this book lists pairs of words that are pronounced similarly (*homonyms*) and are therefore often confused with one another, such as *accept* ("receive") and *except* ("other than"). Word-processing spell checks will not catch these kinds of errors. One instructor's recommendation was that students read their papers aloud before submitting them, as a way of discouraging the kind of skimming that may cause students to miss usage errors.

Another pair of homonyms is *affect* and *effect,* which might still be readily confused even if the student read the paper aloud. However, here are some tips to help you sort out these two homonyms:

◆ In their most common form, *effect* is a noun meaning "outcome" (as in "Aggression is often an *effect* of frustration"), whereas *affect* is a verb meaning "to influence" (as in "The level of frustration *affects* how a person behaves").
◆ However, *effect* can also be used as a verb meaning "to bring about" (as in "The clinical intervention *effected* a measurable improvement").
◆ And *affect* can also be used as a noun meaning "emotion" (as in "Several of the patients participating in this clinical trial exhibited positive *affect*").

Incorrect Use of Singular and Plural

Another potential source of problems is the incorrect use of the singular and plural of some familiar terms. The following shows the correct singular and plural forms:

Singular	Plural
analysis	analyses
anomaly	anomalies
appendix	appendixes or appendices (both are correct)
criterion	criteria
datum	data
hypothesis	hypotheses
phenomenon	phenomena
stimulus	stimuli

For example, one common usage error is the confusion of *phenomena* [plural term] with *phenomenon* [singular term]. It would be incorrect to write, "This [singular pronoun] phenomena [plural subject] is [singular verb] of interest." The correct form is either "This phenomenon is . . ." or "These phenomena are . . ."

Although you will find that words like *data* and *media* are often construed as singular, the general rule is that until there is no question about something's being correct, it is good to be on the safe side (so as not to be criticized by sticklers). In this case, the safe side is to interpret *data* and *media* as plural words. Thus, it would be unsafe to write, "The data [plural subject] indicates [singular verb] . . ." or "The data shows . . ." To be on the safe side, you would write, "The data indicate . . ." or "The data show . . ."

Between and Among

In the past, another common source of confusion was in the use of the words *between* and *among*. We were taught to use *between* when referring to two items only, and to use *among* when there are more than two items. This seems to be a distinction that has gone out of style, however. For example, in the analysis of variance (abbreviated ANOVA), conventional usage says "between sum of squares" and the "between mean square," even if the number of conditions being compared is more than two. *Webster's* (the tenth edition as well as the eleventh edition) denies the correctness of the distinction of the words *between* and *among.*

Prefixes

Other common problems concern the use of some *prefixes* in psychological terms:

◆ The prefix *inter-* means "between" (for example, *interpersonal* means "between persons"); the prefix *intra-* means "within" (for example, *intrapersonal* means "within the person").

◆ The prefix *intro-* means "inward" or "within"; the prefix *extra-* means "outside" or "beyond." The psychological term *introvert* thus refers to an "inner-directed personality"; the term *extravert* indicates an "outer-directed personality."

◆ The prefix *hyper-* means "too much"; the prefix *hypo-* means "too little." Hence, the term *hypothyroidism* refers to a deficiency of thyroid hormone. *Hyperthyroidism* denotes an excess of thyroid hormone, and a *hyperactive* child is one who is excessively active.

Participants versus Subjects

Although not strictly a usage error, referring to human beings who participated in a study as *subjects* is no longer recommended by the APA. Although the term commonly appears in other than APA publications, the reasoning of those who object is that *subjects* sounds passive and nondescriptive, whereas human beings are active agents who initiate as well as react. The APA recommends that writers use *participants* as a general term instead of *subjects,* but that writers also try to be more specific by using terms such as *respondents, children, patients, clients*—depending on the nature or role of those who participated in the study. However, many experimental psychologists still prefer the term *subjects,* and we use both terms (*subjects* and *participants*) in this manual.

Numerals

Another source of bafflement can be the proper use of numerals in the APA style. In general, the APA recommends spelling out single-digit figures (one, two, three, four, five, six, seven, eight, nine) and using figures (10, 20, 30, 40) for numbers with more than one digit. However, there are exceptions to this rule. Here are some guidelines to help you decide when to spell out numbers and when to use figures for numbers:

◆ Although it is recommended that you not begin a sentence with a number, if you must do so, then spell it out ("Twenty-nine students volunteered for this study" or "Fourteen percent of all the participants responded in the affirmative").

- Numbers expressed as words in phrases and sentences should be spelled out (as in "two-tailed test" or the sentence "Only a dozen participants out of 950 refused to go further in the study").
- Spell out *zero* and *one* when they are easier to understand than 0 and 1 ("zero-sum game" or "one-word response").
- When single-digit numbers are part of a numerical group, use figures (for example, "5 of the 25 participants failed to answer this question").
- Use figures for all numbers—even one-digit numbers—that immediately precede a unit of measurement (for example, 3 cm or 9 mg).
- Use figures for units of age and time (4-year-old, 3 months, 2 days, 9 minutes), units of measurement (1 million, 3%), and numbers used in reference lists (pp. 4–6, 2nd ed., Vol. 4).
- Use whatever is the universally accepted style for well-known expressions (the Ten Commandments).

Other APA rules for reporting singular and plural numbers, long sequences of numbers, and physical measurements are the following:

- When reporting the plurals of numbers, add an *s* without an apostrophe. So the plural of 1990 would be 1990s, and the plural of 20 would be 20s.
- Commas are used between groups of three digits (1,000,000), except for page numbers (page 1225), binary digits (001001), serial numbers (345789), degrees of freedom, and numbers to the right of a decimal point (2,300.1357).
- When reporting physical units, use the metric system. For example, 1 foot is reported as .3048 m (or meter, with no period after the *m*), and 1 inch becomes .0254 m. To avoid confusion, you might put a zero before the decimal (0.3048 m or 0.0254 m).

More on Punctuation

Periods

Besides the proper use of commas in reporting numbers, there are various other rules for the use of punctuation marks in your writing. Notice above that there was no period after the *m* for *meter*, because the APA style is not to use a period after a symbol, except when the symbol is at the end of a sentence (a *period* always ends a declarative sentence). Periods are, however, used following an abbreviation other than a physical unit, as in the following common abbreviations of Latin words:

cf.	from *confer* ("compare")
e.g.	from *exempli gratia* ("for example")
et al.	from *et alia* ("and others")
et seq.	from *et sequens* ("and following")

ibid.	from *ibidem* ("in the same place")
i.e.	from *id est* ("that is")
op. cit.	from *opere citato* ("in the work cited")
viz.	from *videlicet* ("namely")

If you continually write *eg.* or *et. al.* in your paper, you will be telling the instructor, I don't know the meaning of these terms! The reason, of course, is that *e.g.* is the abbreviation of two words, not one. Writing *eg.* announces that you believe (mistakenly) it is the abbreviation of one word. Putting a period after *et* tells the instructor that you believe (again, mistakenly) it is an abbreviation, which it is not; it is an entire Latin word.

With the exception of *et al.*, if you use any of these Latin abbreviations, the APA manual requires that they be used only in parentheses and tabular material, and that these abbreviations otherwise be spelled out. As an illustration, take the expression "for example," which you would write as "e.g." and place in parentheses, as in the following:

> Herrnstein and Murray's (1994) book was widely debated (e.g., Andery & Serio, 1997; Andrews & Nelkin, 1996; Carroll, 1997).

Not used in parentheses, it is spelled out rather than abbreviated:

> Herrnstein and Murray's (1994) book was widely debated; see, for example, work by Andery and Serio (1997), Andrews and Nelkin (1996), and Carroll (1997).

The abbreviation *et al.*, however, when used in reference lists and in text, does not have to be in parentheses.

Other abbreviations that are followed by a period are the short forms of English words:

anon.	for *anonymous*
ch.	for *chapter*
diagr.	for *diagram*
ed.	for *editor* or *edition*
fig.	for *figure*
ms.	for *manuscript*
p.	for *page*
pp.	for *pages*
rev.	for *revised*
v.	for *versus* (in references to and text citations of court cases)
vol.	for *volume*
vs.	for *versus, against*

Another important point is that, except for common abbreviations like those above, most abbreviations for terms are first spelled out for the reader.

Thus, in the sample review paper, John writes, ". . . the psychometric idea of a general trait (*g*)," which tells the reader that the abbreviation *g* is defined as a general trait. If you wanted to refer repeatedly to the term *reaction time* or to an instrument called the Humboldt Upside-Down Test, you would write "reaction time (RT)" or "the Humboldt Upside-Down Test (HUDT)" the first time you mentioned the term and then use the abbreviation RT or HUDT whenever you referred to the same term again.

The APA's exception to this rule is that abbreviations that you can find listed as word entries in *Webster's Collegiate Dictionary* do not need to be defined first. For example, the abbreviations IQ, REM, AIDS, HIV, and ESP appear as words in *Webster's* and thus do not need to be defined or set off in parentheses the first time they are used in a psychology paper.

Commas and Semicolons

We mentioned when commas are used and not used in numbers. Some other uses of the *comma* include the following:

- Use commas to separate each of three or more items in a series ("Smith, Jones, and Brown" or "high, medium, and low scorers").
- Use commas to set off introductory phrases in a sentence ("In another experiment performed 10 years later, the same researchers found . . .").
- Use commas to set off thoughts or phrases that are incidental to, or that qualify, the basic idea of the sentence ("This variable, although not part of the researchers' main hypothesis, was also examined").
- Put a comma before coordinating conjunctions (*and, but, or, nor, yet*) when they join independent clauses ("The subject lost weight, but he was still able to . . .").

A common error is to insert a comma before a transitional expression such as *however, moreover,* or *therefore* when it is used to connect two complete clauses in a compound sentence. For example, "The participants voiced no concerns, however, it was quite obvious that they were uncomfortable" clearly consists of two complete clauses. Instead of a comma before *however,* a *semicolon* (;) should be used. Alternatively, this compound sentence can easily be divided into two sentences: "The participants voiced no concerns. However, it was quite obvious that they were uncomfortable." Still another alternative is to replace the transitional expression *however* with the conjunction *but* preceded by a comma: The participants voiced no concerns, but it was quite obvious that they were uncomfortable.

As a general rule, a semicolon is called for when the thoughts in the two independent clauses are close, and the writer wishes to emphasize this closeness or to contrast the two thoughts. The following is an example of the appropriate use of a semicolon for connecting thoughts:

> Anorexia nervosa is a disorder in which the victims literally starve themselves; despite their emaciated appearance, they consider themselves overweight.

In most instances, however, these long sentences can be divided into shorter ones, which will be clearer:

> Anorexia nervosa is a disorder in which the victims literally starve themselves. Despite their emaciated appearance, they consider themselves overweight.

The Colon

Generally, the *colon* (:) is used to indicate that a list will follow, or to introduce an amplification. The colon tells the reader, "Note what follows."

Here is an example in which we see a colon used to indicate that a list follows:

> Subjects were given the following items: (a) four calling birds, (b) three French hens, (c) two turtle doves . . .

An example of the amplification use of a colon is the title of Jane Doe's research report. Another example of amplification would be

> Gardner (1983) postulated two forms of the personal intelligences: interpersonal and intrapersonal intelligence.

For another use of the colon, observe in the reference lists of the two sample papers at the end of this book that a colon is inserted between the place of publication of a book and the name of the publisher—for example, "Belmont, CA: Wadsworth" or "Boston: McGraw-Hill" or "Upper Saddle River, NJ: Prentice Hall" or "Mahwah, NJ: Erlbaum." We will have more to say about the punctuation used in references in the next chapter.

Punctuation in Quoted Passages

We mentioned the ellipsis mark (. . .) used in quoted passages to indicate that selected words have been intentionally omitted. You will sometimes also see in quoted passages brackets ([ ]) with words inside them. The use of brackets tells us that the words are not part of the original quotation but were inserted by the writer who is using this quoted material. For example, omitting some words might make a quoted passage seem grammatically incorrect or might make something unclear, but either of these problems can be easily fixed by the insertion of a few connecting words in brackets.

Earlier, we also mentioned the importance of putting quotation marks around words that are quoted. An exception is when a quotation is 40 or more words, in which case it is set off from the body of the text by means of indented margins, and quotation marks are omitted. However, if there is an internal quotation within the longer quotation, then *double quotation marks* (". . .") are inserted around the quote within a quote, as in the following example:

What practical implications did Rosenthal and Jacobson (1968) draw from their research findings? They wrote:

> As teacher-training institutions begin to teach the possibility that teachers' expectations of their pupils' performance may serve as self-fulfilling prophecies, there may be a new expectancy created. The new expectancy may be that children can learn more than had been believed possible, an expectation held by many educational theorists, though for quite different reasons. . . . The new expectancy, at the very least, will make it more difficult when they encounter the educationally disadvantaged for teachers to think, "Well, after all, what can you expect?" The man [*sic*] on the street may be permitted his opinions and prophecies of the unkempt children loitering in a dreary schoolyard. The teacher in the schoolroom may need to learn that those same prophecies within her [*sic*] may be fulfilled; she is no casual passer-by. Perhaps Pygmalion in the classroom is more her role. (pp. 181–182)

When a quoted passage is fewer than 40 words, double quotation marks are used and the passage is simply inserted in the text as part of the narrative. If there is a smaller quote within the quoted passage, then *single quotation marks* ('. . .') are used to set off the quote within a quote, as in the following sentence:

> Participant B responded, "My feeling about this difficult situation was summed up in a nutshell by Jim when he said, 'It's a tough job, but somebody has to do it.'"

As this example also illustrates, if the appropriate punctuation is a period (as shown at the end of this sentence), it is included *within* the quotation marks. The same rule applies to a comma; it is inserted within the quotation marks. But if the appropriate punctuation is a colon or a semicolon, it is inserted *after* the closing quotation marks.

In the lengthy quote above, which begins, "As teacher-training institutions . . ." and ends ". . . in the classroom is more her role," notice that the numbers of the pages on which the passage appears in Rosenthal and Jacobson's book are shown in parentheses at the end. Notice also that the word *sic* (Latin, meaning "thus") is inserted in brackets in two places; it indicates that a word or phrase that appears strange or incorrect is quoted verbatim. Thus, if you wanted to make the point that a quoted passage ignores gender, you would insert in brackets the word *sic* as shown. But observe that we did not insert *sic* after every gender term. In the first sentence, the masculine pronoun *his* was not set off by *sic* because the reference is "man on the street." In the second sentence, the feminine pronoun *she* is also not set off, because the referent is "within her."

Revising and Polishing

In the next chapter, we consider the details of producing the final manuscript. Revising and polishing the draft of your paper are best done after you have been able to leave the manuscript alone for a while. When you approach your writing after having taken such a break (ideally, 24 hours or more), your critical powers will be sharper. Syntax errors, lapses in logic, and other problems will become evident, so smoothing out these sections will be a relatively simple chore.

As you reread and polish your writing, consider the following suggestions:

◆ Be concise.
◆ Break up long paragraphs that contain a lot of disparate ideas into smaller, more coherent paragraphs.
◆ Be specific.
◆ Choose words for what they mean, not just for how they sound.
◆ Double-check punctuation.
◆ Don't use a long word when a short word will do.
◆ Don't be redundant (for example, "most unique" is redundant).
◆ Don't let spelling errors mar your writing.
◆ If you are unsure about how to spell a word, use the spell-check function on your word processor; if the answer you get seems ambiguous, check your dictionary.

If you are new to word processing (or are learning a new word-processing program), be sure you know how to save and back up your work when you are ready to start composing and revising. A good system will do these tasks for you automatically at regular intervals, but you must specify the interval you want. You never know when the electricity will suddenly go out or someone will playfully or accidentally hit a wrong key, or you yourself might be distracted and hit a wrong key and send your latest work into oblivion.

Making a backup means not only storing something inside the computer's hard drive (that is, if it's *your* PC) but also copying it onto a floppy disk, a ZIP disk, or a CD. Our habit is also to make a printout every few days. Having a printed copy will allow you to inspect and modify the layout to make sure it looks the way you want it to. It also allows you to polish your writing in a format that is tangible. Sometimes spelling errors and murky passages that are less apparent on-screen jump out as your eye traverses a printed page.

8

PRODUCING THE
FINAL MANUSCRIPT

*This chapter provides you with guidelines and tips for producing
a finished product. The layout and production of your final
manuscript are like the icing on a cake. If the underlying
structure is sound, the result will be smooth and predictable.*

General Pointers

Writing on a computer means that the steps involved in first drafts, revisions, and final drafts are telescoped. These stages lose their formal definition because the computer allows you, with the stroke of a key or the click of a mouse, to shift or change words, sentences, paragraphs, and even entire sections as you compose and revise. In the old days, when students could use only a typewriter, it was painfully difficult to revise, because they had to equip themselves with scissors and glue to literally cut and paste and then each time had to retype those sections of the paper that had been changed. Notes, long quotations, references, tables, and figures that you will need for your final draft can be stored in your computer's memory or on a disk and can be retrieved as needed. The computer is not a substitute for the hard work of organizing your ideas, thinking them through, and expressing them clearly, but it releases you from an enormous amount of drudgery.

Word-processing systems have spelling checkers and grammar checkers, which are designed to flag mistakes, offer alternatives, and let you choose whether to make a particular change or to ignore the alternative recommendations. These programs are not infallible, so do not let them lull you into a false sense of security or into thinking that they are a substitute for careful proofreading of your final manuscript. Your spelling checker is based on a dictionary (actually a word inventory) in the word-processing system, but many technical terms that psychologists and other professionals use may not appear in your word-processing inventory. If your spelling checker flags a word that you know is spelled correctly, add the correct spelling to the word inventory. Notice that there are lists of commonly misspelled words on the inside front and back covers of this manual; if you peruse this list once you have written a first draft of your proposal or final paper, some words may stand out as possible mistakes in your paper that the spelling checker missed.

Grammar checkers are designed to flag a sentence that violates a particular grammar or style rule. When it encounters what it has been programmed to define as a problem, a grammar dialog box appears on the screen, and you are asked whether you want to accept a suggestion or ignore it. You can set up the word processor so that the grammar checker automatically searches for violations as you write and flags them as they are encountered, or you can simply turn off the grammar checker and use it only when you want it. As many experienced writers know, grammar checkers can be maddening because they often "catch" acceptable stylistic variations and fail to recognize stylistic requirements that may have been violated. Although it is essential to keep the spelling checker active, many writers prefer not to use the grammar checker and instead depend on their own eyes and experience to catch mistakes and correct them.

Another useful tool in your word-processing system is the thesaurus, which you access by clicking on the appropriate menu option (or right-clicking in Word 98 or later versions, and then opening on the Synonyms submenu). The thesaurus in your word-processing system looks up synonyms for words or phrases, and you then choose whether to replace a word with one of the synonyms. However, you need to make sure that the replacement word means the same thing as your original word, a decision that only you can make. If you are not absolutely sure, look up the replacement word in your dictionary.

Here are more general pointers as you set about producing the final manuscript:

- ◆ Make sure the type is legible. If it is faint, invest in a new ink cartridge.
- ◆ Use double line spacing, and print on only one side of the sheet of paper, inserting a page header in the upper right corner and numbering pages as the two sample papers illustrate.
- ◆ Make a second copy of the finished paper. The original is for your instructor, and the duplicate copy will ensure the immediate availability of an exact spare copy in case of an unforeseen problem.
- ◆ Don't format your word processor to create a justified (even) right margin, which produces a block effect and, sometimes, odd spacing within lines. Instead, let the right margin remain ragged (uneven), as the APA manual stipulates.
- ◆ Use a 12-point typeface, preferably Times New Roman or Courier, both of which are known as *serif typefaces,* so called because of the tiny line that finishes off a main stroke of a letter. If you are lettering drawings and figures, however, use a typeface without a serif (called *sans serif typefaces*) because it provides a sharper visual presentation in graphics.

◆ Don't use the letter *l* to represent the numeral one or the letter *o* to represent a zero; instead use the separate 1 and 0 keys for these digits. Also, don't use *X* to represent chi; instead, insert the proper symbol (χ) by using the appropriate submenu, or else write it in by hand.

◆ The style recommended by the APA for manuscripts submitted for publication is to use one space following all punctuation, including the space between sentences. However, if you are in the habit of inserting two spaces after a period (which we are), do what is comfortable. (The APA does not reject manuscripts on the basis of the spacing around punctuation.)

We turn now to other specifics of layout and processing that will help to give your finished paper a pleasing appearance.

Title Page Format

Glance at the title pages of the two sample papers at the end of this book. The title summarizes the main idea of the project and is centered on the page. (Notice that the title appears again on page 3 of each sample paper.) A good title is succinct and yet adequately describes to the reader the gist of the work. You will already have arrived at a working title when narrowing your topic and drafting a proposal (Chapter Three). That title can now be changed or made more specific if you feel it is no longer accurate or completely descriptive of the finished product. (Incidentally, the APA style is to capitalize prepositions of four or more letters in titles and headings, so you would capitalize *With* or *From* if it appears in the title of your paper.)

Other information is also shown on the title page of these sample papers:

The page header and page number
The student's name (called the *byline*)
The student's e-mail address or other contact information
The number and name of the course or sequence for which the paper was written
The instructor's or adviser's name
The date the paper will be submitted

The page number in the upper-right corner is accompanied (on every page) by one or more words. These words are called *page headers,* and their purpose is to make it easy for the reader to identify each manuscript page if some pages become separated from the rest. Most word-processing programs make it easy enough to insert a page header. As you revise—cutting and pasting—the word processor will automatically update the page numbers.

Showing the instructor's name (if the paper is submitted for a course) or the adviser's name (if the paper is submitted to fulfill some other requirement, such as a "prelim" paper) is a courtesy. If the paper is a thesis, another courtesy is to include an acknowledgment page (after the title page) on which you thank your adviser and any others who extended a helping hand as you worked on your project. Incidentally, theses also usually include a table of contents page.

Headings

It is customary to break up the text of a lengthy paper with brief but informative headings. One purpose of these headings is to provide a conceptual map that enables readers to understand exactly where they are as they examine the sequence of topics or issues discussed in the paper. Another purpose is to organize the writer's thinking, so that topics that belong in one section do not accidentally stray into another section where they do not belong. A third purpose is to shepherd readers through the logical flow of the paper, from the most important to the least important (but still relevant) topics, issues, or information.

If you are writing a review paper, a thesis, or some other kind of term paper, you should be able to derive these headings from the outline of your paper or thesis. Observe, for example, how John Smith's headings and subheadings lend symmetry to his review paper, showing its progressive development in concise phrases. John's paper uses two formats of headings: center and flush left. *Center headings* are used to separate the paper into major sections, are written in uppercase and lowercase letters, and are not italicized (or underlined):

Two General Conceptions of Intelligence
Gardner's Theory of Multiple Intelligences
Two Main Criticisms of Multiplex Theories
Conclusions

To subdivide these major sections, John uses *subheadings* that are flush left, in italics, and in uppercase and lowercase. John uses three subheadings to partition the major section labeled "Gardner's Theory of Multiple Intelligences":

Gardner's Notion of Intelligence
Many Kinds of Intelligence
Independence of Abilities

If he had needed to use a second level of subheadings, they would be indented, italicized, and followed by a period, with the body of the text immediately following the subheading. For example, they might look like the following if he had wanted to partition the section labeled *"Many Kinds of Intelligence"* and had begun with a *"Logical-Mathematical"* subheading:

Many Kinds of Intelligence
   Logical-Mathematical. One traditional type of intelligence, called
"logical-mathematical" by Gardner (1985), refers to . . .

If you are writing a research report, you simply use headings that are inherent in the structure of virtually all research reports in psychology when only a single study or experiment is reported. In Jane Doe's research report, under the major heading of "Method," she uses *"Participants"* and *"Procedure"* as subheadings to partition this section. Had she then subdivided these two subsections, she would have used the second-level subheading that we described above (i.e., indented, italicized, and ended by a period, with the text immediately following). There are further levels of subheadings used by writers preparing more lengthy or complex manuscripts, but the ones illustrated here should suffice for students writing review papers and research reports.

Italicizing

Before the days of word processors, underlining was used to indicate to typesetters that selected text was to be set in italics. Nowadays, it is a simple matter to format text in italics; you just click and type, or you highlight and click. The APA does not object, however, if authors of manuscripts submitted for publication use underlining rather than italics, because once a paper is accepted for publication, the copy editor inserts an underline anyway. Conventional usage also calls for the titles of books mentioned in the body of the text to be italicized ("In *Pygmalion in the Classroom*, Rosenthal and Jacobson wrote that . . .").

Italicizing is also used in several other ways:

◆ Letters used as statistical symbols are italicized: F, N, n, P, p, t, Z, and so forth. Note that some symbols are in lowercase, and this can be very important. For example, an uppercase N indicates the total number of sampling units, and a lowercase n indicates the number of units in a subsample of N.

◆ However, Greek letters used as statistical symbols are not italicized—for example, the symbol for chi-square (χ^2), the symbol instructing us to sum a set of scores (Σ), the symbol for the standard deviation of a population of scores (σ), and the symbol for the variance of a population of scores (σ^2).

◆ In reference lists, volume numbers of journal articles and titles of books and journals are italicized.

◆ Words that you wish to emphasize are italicized, but this device should be used sparingly ("Effective teaching, the authors asserted, will come only from the teachers' firm belief that their pupils *can* perform").

◆ Words used to illustrate are also italicized ("the term *knowing* . . ." or ". . . is called *knowing*"). For example, John Smith writes, "People use the word *intelligence* and its various synonyms . . ." and "The second major view . . . is characterized here as the *multiplex view* because . . .").

Rarely do students need to insert into a paper a statistical formula with superscripts and subscripts. Unless you are using a program (such as MathType) that gives you the option of italicizing each unit of a formula, it can be inconvenient to try to selectively italicize parts of the formula. One option is to use the equation editor function and let it go at that. Another option is to write the formula by hand. If you are inserting formulas into the appendix of your research report, you can either type them (as shown in Jane's report; she used MathType for formulas) or write them out by hand.

Citations in Text

There are several simple conventions for citing an author's work in the narrative text of a paper. The purpose of a citation is to make it easy for the reader to identify the source of a quotation or an idea and then to locate the particular reference in the list at the end of the paper. The author-date method is the format stipulated in the APA manual. The surname of the author and the year of publication are inserted in the text at the appropriate point.

Here are two general rules and the exceptions:

◆ Do not list any publication in your reference list that you do not cite. The exception to this rule would be if you were developing an extensive bibliography of references and wanted to list every relevant article and book on the subject, whether you discussed it in your manuscript or not. Of course, you would not be expected to compile such a bibliography for a review paper or a research report in a course.

◆ Do not cite any source material in the text without placing it in the reference list. The exception to this rule is a personal communication cited in the text, because it is unnecessary to put it in the list of references as well.

If you want to cite a source that you did not read yourself, make it clear that you are using someone else's citation (called a *secondary citation*). Use a secondary source only if the original source is unavailable to you; otherwise examine and cite the original source yourself. The reason to refrain from using secondary sources is that there is no guarantee that the material you want to cite is described correctly in the secondary source. However, as one instructor recently reminded us, community college libraries and other small libraries may not provide direct access to all of the primary sources needed by students. In general, sources may be cited in the text in two ways: as part of the narrative and in parentheses (in alphabetical order, and then by year if the same author is cited twice).

If you must use a secondary source for information that you did not read in the original form, here is the way to cite it in the text:

Citation of Secondary Source as Part of Text

In Virgil's epic poem, *The Aeneid* (as cited in Allport & Postman, 1947), the following characterization of Fama appears: . . .

Here is an example of two different citations of two secondary sources in the narrative text:

Citations of Secondary Sources

Hasher, Goldstein, and Toppino's finding (as cited in Kendzierski & Markey, 2002) is also consistent with the traditional idea that merely being exposed over and over to the same propaganda, even if it is blatantly false, is usually enough to instill confidence in its credibility (McCullough, Murphy, & Schwartz, 1911, as cited in Fraites, 2004).

Notice in the example above that the word *and* is spelled out in the narrative citation, but an ampersand (&) is used in the parenthetical citation. Here are two further examples of this use, both primary citations:

Citation Appearing as Part of Text

Baldwin, Doyle, Hooper, Mithalal, and Stella (1991) asked a sample of child-care providers to describe incidents in which . . .

Citation Entirely in Parentheses

Institutional review boards may harbor quite different biases regarding the ethical risks of the studies they are asked to evaluate (e.g., Ceci, Peters, & Plotkin, 1985; Hamsher & Reznikoff, 1967; Kallgren & Kenrick, 1990; Schlenker & Forsyth, 1977).

These examples also illustrate the convention of author-date citations that dictates the listing of the surnames of up to six authors the first time the citation is given. In subsequent citations, if there are more than two authors, you give the surname of only the first author, followed by *et al.* and the date (Baldwin et al., 1997). Here are two more examples:

Subsequent Citation as Part of Text

Ceci et al. (1985) found that one research proposal, approved without changes in one institution, was amended at another institution in the same city.

Subsequent Citation Entirely in Parentheses

One research proposal, approved without changes in one institution, was amended at another institution in the same city (Ceci et al., 1985).

To cite an e-mail message or a written communication you have received, you would refer to it as a personal communication, but (as previously mentioned) you would not list it again in your references section:

Personal Communication as Part of Text

An alternative approach, noted by T. E. Schoenfelder (personal communication, August 12, 2004), would explain investment decisions within the framework of behavioral decision theory.

Personal Communication in Parentheses

An alternative approach would explain investment decisions within the framework of behavioral decision theory (T. E. Schoenfelder, personal communication, August 12, 2004).

To cite a specific document obtained from a Web site, you would use a format similar to that for printed material (as shown above). If all you want is to cite a particular Web site but not a specific document from that Web site, you would give the address of the site but not include it in your references section:

Web Site Citation

Information about the *Publication Manual of the American Psychological Association* (5th ed.) can be found on the *APA Publication Manual* Web site (http://www.apastyle.org).

Here are some other specific rules that cover most of the cases that students encounter:

◆ If you are citing a series of works, the proper sequence is alphabetical order by the surname of the first author and then by chronological order (Brecher, 1999; DiClemente, 2000; DiFonzo & Bordia, 1993; Frei, 2002; Freeman, 1999; Gergen & Shotter, 1985, 1988; Stern, in press; Strohmetz, 1997; Trimble, in press; Wells & Lafleur, 1997).

◆ Two or more works published by the same author in the same year are designated as *a, b, c,* and so on (Hantula, 2001a, 2001b, 2001c). In the references section, the alphabetical order of the works' titles determines the sequence when there is more than one work by an author in the same year.

◆ Work accepted for publication but not yet printed is designated *in press* (Crabb, in press); in a list of citations, the rule is to place this work last: (Crabb, 2000, 2001, in press).

What should you do if you run into a problem that these rules do not address? You might check out the APA Web site. However, even the APA seems quite flexible and does not return manuscripts simply because the format of one unusual citation deviates from the norm. Once the manuscript is accepted for publication, corrections are made during the copyediting process. Thus, keep one general idea in mind as you go beyond these specific guidelines: If you run into a problem, ask yourself whether you could identify a reference based on the citation you have provided. In other words, put yourself in your reader's shoes, but also try to be consistent.

Tables and Figures

As discussed earlier in this book, tables and figures can be used to augment the presentation of the results. Often, however, when students include tables in their research reports, they are merely presenting their raw data in a neat format. Save your raw data for the appendix of your report (if your raw data are required), as shown in Jane's report. Keep in mind that statistical tables in results sections of research reports are intended to *summarize* the raw data rather than to present the actual data (see Jane's Table 1); tables can also summarize other results (see Jane's Table 2, which summarizes her ANOVA and linear contrast results).

The APA requires that tables and figures, numbered in the order in which they are first mentioned in the paper, be put on separate pages at the end of the paper (in the case of student papers, the "end of the paper" is defined as the section after the list of references but before the appendix). Notice that the titles of the tables in Jane's report appear above the tables. If these were figures instead of tables, then the title (called the *caption*) would appear below the figure in the printed article, and the word *Figure* and the number of the figure would be in italics. When a paper is submitted to a journal, even the figure captions are placed on a separate page, apart from the figures themselves.

These requirements can get confusing for students who are writing research reports for a course. To simplify this situation, just insert the caption below the figure. For example, if, instead of a table, Jane had used a figure showing a bar graph, the caption below the figure might look like this:

Figure 1. A bar diagram showing the mean tip percentages in four treatment conditions. The standard deviations in these four conditions were 1.46, 1.71, 2.45, and 2.43, respectively, and the sample size was 20 per condition.

As you can see, there is a lot of information crammed into this caption. All this information was neatly condensed in Jane's Table 1 in her final report (in Appendix A), which also lists the mean tip percentages to two decimal places (so it is easy for a curious reader to recalculate her test statistics).

If you are using tables, notice that Jane's table titles, in uppercase and lowercase letters, are flush left and italicized. Each column of a table is expected to have a heading, including the left-most column (called the *stub column*, it usually lists the major independent variables). Column headings identify the items below them, and some tables use a hierarchy of headings (known as *decked heads*) to avoid repeating words. When the top heading in the hierarchy spans the body of the table, it is called a *table spanner*. But these are technical details. Just remember to keep your table headings clear, concise, and informative, so the reader can easily understand what is in the table.

If you are still confused about the difference between a table and a figure, think of figures as bar graphs and line graphs. Graphics that are photographed or imported from artwork are also considered figures. As we mentioned earlier, because figures can introduce distortions that detract from a clear, concise summary of the data, most researchers prefer to use tables when giving summary details (group means and standard deviations, for example). If you must use a figure, be sure not to overcomplicate it. The basic rule is to use only figures that add to the text and do not repeat what you can say very clearly in words. (If you are interested in learning about the psychology and art of graphic design, see the recommended readings at the end of Chapter Six.)

If you need to add some clarifying or explanatory information to a table, it is customary to place this information below the table, as illustrated in Jane's report. The word *Note* is in italics with a period, and the information follows. To add a few specific notes to a table, the convention is to use superscript lowercase letters (a, b, c) or asterisks (*,**, ***). The following cases illustrate this usage:

Superscript Notation

$^a n = 50$ $\qquad$ $^b n = 62$

Asterisk Notation

$^* p < .05$ $\qquad$ $^{**} p < .01$ $\qquad$ $^{***} p < .0005$

List of References

The list of references starts on a new page, with the title "References" centered at the top of the page. The references are arranged alphabetically by the surname of the first author and then by the date of publication. Prefixes (von, Mc, Mac, de, du, for example) can give students pause as they try to figure out how to alphabetize them, and the APA manual has specific rules based on whether or not the prefix is customarily used when the person is referred to. Rather than wrestle with these nuances, simply alphabetize by the prefix when you add such names to your list of references.

The standard style rules of the APA manual are to:

◆ Invert all authors' names (that is, last name, first initial, middle initial).
◆ List authors' names in the exact order in which they appear on the title page of the publication.
◆ Use commas to separate authors and an ampersand (&) before the last author.
◆ Give the year the work was copyrighted (the year and month for magazine articles and the year, month, and day for newspaper articles).
◆ In titles of books, chapters in books, and journal articles, capitalize only the first word of the title and of the subtitle (if any) as well as any proper names.
◆ Give the issue number of the journal if the article cited is paginated by issue.
◆ Italicize the volume number of a journal article and the title of a book or a journal.
◆ Give the city and state of a book's publisher, using the postal abbreviations listed in Exhibit 15.

EXHIBIT 15 *Postal abbreviations for states and territories*

Location	Abbreviation	Location	Abbreviation
Alabama	AL	Montana	MT
Alaska	AK	Nebraska	NE
Arizona	AZ	Nevada	NV
Arkansas	AR	New Hampshire	NH
California	CA	New Jersey	NJ
Colorado	CO	New Mexico	NM
Connecticut	CT	New York	NY
Delaware	DE	North Carolina	NC
District of Columbia	DC	North Dakota	ND
Florida	FL	Ohio	OH
Georgia	GA	Oklahoma	OK
Guam	GU	Oregon	OR
Hawaii	HI	Pennsylvania	PA
Idaho	ID	Puerto Rico	PR
Illinois	IL	Rhode Island	RI
Indiana	IN	South Carolina	SC
Iowa	IA	South Dakota	SD
Kansas	KS	Tennessee	TN
Kentucky	KY	Texas	TX
Louisiana	LA	Utah	UT
Maine	ME	Vermont	VT
Maryland	MD	Virginia	VA
Massachusetts	MA	Virgin Islands	VI
Michigan	MI	Washington	WA
Minnesota	MN	West Virginia	WV
Mississippi	MS	Wisconsin	WI
Missouri	MO	Wyoming	WY

◆ However, major cities in the United States (such as Baltimore, Boston, Chicago, Dallas, Los Angeles, New York, Philadelphia, and San Francisco) can be listed without a state abbreviation.

◆ If you are listing a foreign city other than Amsterdam, Jerusalem, London, Milan, Moscow, New Delhi, Paris, Rome, Stockholm, Tokyo, or Vienna, include the country as well.

Using these rules and the notes and examples below, you should encounter few problems. If you experience a problem, you might be able to generalize from these rules and notes or find an answer on the *APA Publication Manual* Web site (http://www.apastyle.org). Remember that the APA rule of thumb in all cases is to be clear, consistent, and complete in referencing source material:

Authored Book

Single author
Invert the author's name, using initials for the first and middle names, and give the year of publication, the italicized title of the book (capitalizing the first word of the title and subtitle), and the location and name of the publisher.

> Kimmel, A. J. (1996). *Ethical issues in behavioral research: A survey.* Cambridge, MA: Blackwell.

More than one author
Same as above, but insert a comma followed by an ampersand (&) before the last author's name.

> Shadish, W. R., Cook, T. D., & Campbell, D. T. (2001). *Experimental and quasi-experimental designs for generalized causal inference.* Boston: Houghton Mifflin.

Institutional author and publisher the same
Give the full name of the institution, and list the publisher's name as "Author" when it is the same as the institutional author.

> American Psychiatric Association. (1994). *Diagnostic and statistical manual of mental disorders* (4th ed.). Washington, DC: Author.

Work in Press

Edited volume in production but not yet published
An edited volume that has been accepted by the publisher and is presumed to be in the process of production is considered in press. Insert in parentheses the abbreviation "Ed." (if one editor) or "Eds." (if more than one editor), followed by a period, and then write in press in parentheses, followed by a period.

> Wilson, B., & Pierce-Haven, J. (Eds.). (in press). *Theories of perception in experimental psychology: Classic and contemporary contributions.* Belmont, CA: Brooks/Cole.

Journal article accepted for publication but not yet in print
A journal article is considered in press if it has been officially accepted for publication by the editor of a journal, but not if it has merely been submitted to a journal.

> Frei, R. L., Racicot, B., & Travagline, A. (in press). The impact of monochromic and type A behavior patterns on faculty research productivity and job-induced stress. *Journal of Managerial Psychology.*

Chapter in edited book in production but not yet in print
A chapter that has been accepted by the editor of a book that, in turn, has been accepted by the publisher is considered in press. Notice that the editors' names are not inverted, whereas the chapter authors' names are inverted as usual.

> Suls, J., & Martin, R. (in press). Social comparison processes in the physical health domain. In A. Baum, T. Revenson, & J. Singer (Eds.), *Handbook of health and psychology.* Mahwah, NJ: Erlbaum.

Authored book in production but not yet in print
A book manuscript that has been accepted by a publisher and is in the process of being prepared for publication is considered in press. Notice that the state as well as the city are listed in this illustration, the reason being that there is also a Cambridge in the United Kingdom.

> Fine, G. A. (in press). *Mushroom worlds: Naturework and the taming of the wild.* Cambridge, MA: Harvard University Press.

Monograph in a journal issue not yet in print
A monograph is a lengthy manuscript that the journal publishes either separately as a supplement or as an entire issue of the journal. This example refers to a monograph accepted by the editor, but not yet printed; once the monograph is published, the issue number and the supplement or part number (if it is published separately) are indicated in parentheses after the volume number.

> Lana, R. E. (in press). Choice and chance in the formation of society. *Journal of Mind and Behavior.*

Edited Published Work

Single editor of a book
After the editor's name, insert "Ed." in parentheses, followed by a period, the italicized title of the book, and so forth.

> Morawski, J. G. (Ed.). (1988). *The rise of experimentation in American psychology.* New Haven, CT: Yale University Press.

More than one editor, more than one volume, revised edition
To indicate more than one editor, "Eds." is inserted in parentheses, followed by a period. The number of the edition and the number of volumes (and the abbreviation "Vols.," capitalized) are noted in parentheses after the title. For the first revised edition, the abbreviation "Rev. ed." can be substituted for "2nd ed."

> Gilbert, D. T., Fiske, S. T., & Lindzey, G. (Eds.). (1988). *The handbook of social psychology* (4th ed., Vols. 1–2). Boston: McGraw-Hill.

Work Republished at a Later Date

Book of collected work
The date that the original work appeared is included in parentheses after the full citation of the current edition.

> Demosthenes. (1852). *The Olynthiac and other public orations of Demosthenes.* London: Henry G. Bohn. (Original work written 349 B.C.)

Single volume in multivolume series of collected work
The years in parentheses (1779/1971) indicate that the original work was published in 1779 and the current edition in 1971; the number of the particular volume in which the work appeared is indicated in parentheses after the title of the series.

> Lessing, G. E. (1779/1971). *Gotthold Ephraim Lessing: Werke* (Vol. 2). München, Germany: Carl Hanser Verlag.

Chapter in an anthology
The years in parentheses (1733/1903) indicate the date of publication of the original work and the anthology. The pages on which the work appears in the anthology are indicated in parentheses after the title of the anthology, followed by a period.

> Pope, A. (1733/1903). Moral essays: Epistle I. To Sir Richard Temple, Lord Cobham, of the knowledge and character of men. In H. W. Boynton (Ed.), *The complete poetical works of Pope* (pp. 157–160). Boston: Houghton Mifflin.

Article or Chapter

Article by a single author in journal paginated by volume
The journal name and volume *(42)* are written in italics, followed by the page numbers (97–108, not in italics) of the article.

> Scott-Jones, D. (1994). Ethical issues in reporting and referring in research with low-income minority children. *Ethics and Behavior, 42,* 97–108.

Article by up to six authors in journal paginated by volume
An ampersand (&) is placed before the last author's name, and only the journal name and volume are italicized.

> Gabrieli, J. D. E., Fleischman, D. A., Keane, M. M., Reminger, S. L., & Morrell, F. (1995). Double dissociation between memory systems underlying explicit and implicit memory in the human brain. *Psychological Science, 6,* 76–82.

More than six authors

If there are seven or more authors, only the first six are listed, followed by a comma and "et al." (no ampersand).

> Thomas, C. B., Hall, J. A., Miller, F. D., Dewhirst, J. R., Fine, G. A., Taylor, M., et al. (1979). Evaluation apprehension, social desirability, and the interpretation of test correlations. *Social Behavior and Personality, 7,* 193–197.

Chapter in edited book

The authors' names are inverted, but not the editors' names. The page numbers of the chapter (pp. 130–165) are placed in parentheses immediately after the italicized title of the book, followed by a period.

> Aditya, R. N., House, R. J., & Kerr, S. (2000). Theory and practice of leadership: Into the new millennium. In C. L. Cooper & E. A. Locke (Eds.), *Industrial and organizational psychology: Linking theory and practice* (pp. 130–165). Cambridge, MA: Blackwell.

Chapter author with hyphenated first and last names

Hyphens in the first name and last name are retained, with all other information presented as before.

> Perret-Clermont, A.-N., Perret, J.-F., & Bell, N. (1991). The social construction of meaning and cognitive ability in elementary school children. In L. Resnick, J. M. Levine, & S. B. Teasley (Eds.), *Perspectives on socially shared cognition* (pp. 41–62). Washington, DC: American Psychological Association.

Entry in encyclopedia paginated by volume

The volume and page numbers of the entry are indicated in parentheses after the italicized title of the encyclopedia. Unusual in this example is that there were two publishers of the encyclopedia, both (as indicated) located in the same city.

> Stanley, J. C. (1971). Design of controlled experiments in education. In L. C. Deighton (Ed.), *The encyclopedia of education* (Vol. 3, pp. 474–483). New York: Macmillan and Free Press.

Article in newsletter paginated by issue

Immediately after the italicized volume number *(23),* the issue number is indicated (4, no italics) in parentheses.

> Camara, W. J. (2001). Do accommodations improve or hinder psychometric qualities of assessment? *The Score Newsletter, 23*(4), 4–6.

Article in journal paginated by issue
Same as above.

> Valdiserri, R. O., Tama, G. M., & Ho, M. (1988). The role of community advisory committees in clinical trials of anti-HIV agents. *IRB: A Review of Human Subjects Research, 10*(4), 5–7.

Non-English Publication

Book
Diacritical marks (an umlaut in *Störeffekte* in this example) and capital letters are used for non-English words in the same way they were used in the original language. The English translation of the book's title is included in brackets immediately after the German title, followed by a period.

> Gniech, G. (1976). *Störeffekte in psychologischen Experimenten* [Artifacts in psychological experiments]. Stuttgart, Germany: Verlag W. Kohlhammer.

Journal article
The same rule referring to the use of diacritical marks and capital letters applies to the non-English title of the article and the name of the journal.

> Foa, U. G. (1966). Le nombre huit dans la socialization de l'enfant [The number eight in the socialization of the infant]. *Bulletin du Centre d'Études et Recherches Psychologiques, 15,* 39–47.

Chapter in Multivolume Edited Series

Different author and editor
Volume and page numbers of the chapter are indicated in parentheses after the italicized series title.

> Kipnis, D. (1984). The use of power in organizations and interpersonal settings. In S. Oskamp (Ed.), *Applied social psychology* (Vol. 5, pp. 171–210). Newbury Park, CA: Sage.

Same author and editor
Notice that the chapter author's name is inverted, but the same name is not inverted when the author is also the editor of the series in which the chapter appears.

> Koch, S. (1959). General introduction to the series. In S. Koch (Ed.), *Psychology: A study of a science* (Vol. 1, pp. 1–18). New York: McGraw-Hill.

Mass Media Article

Magazine article

In parentheses followed by a period, the year and month(s) (if published monthly) and the day (if published more frequently than monthly) are indicated. If the volume number is known, then it is indicated as shown here in italics *(29)*, followed by the page numbers.

> Csikszentmihalyi, M. (1996, July/August). The creative personality. *Psychology Today, 29,* 36–40.

Newspaper article (author listed)

All the page numbers are indicated for an article that appears on discontinuous pages, and the page numbers are separated by a comma.

> Grady, D. (1999, October 11). Too much of a good thing? Doctor challenges drug manual. *The New York Times,* Section F, pp. 1, 2.

Newspaper article (no author listed)

When no author's name is listed in a newspaper article, the work is referenced by the title of the article and alphabetized in the list of references by the first significant word in the title ("toast").

> A toast to Newton and a long-lived "Principia." (1999, October 11). *The New York Times,* Section F, p. 4.

Dictionary or Encyclopedia

Dictionary (no author listed)

When no author's name is listed on the title page of a dictionary or an encyclopedia, the work is referenced by the title of the work and alphabetized by the first significant word in the title.

> *Random House dictionary of the English language.* (1966). New York: Random House.

Encyclopedia (more than one volume, two publishers in two locations)

After the name of the general editor of the encyclopedia, "Ed." is inserted in parentheses, followed by a period. The number of volumes appears in parentheses following the title; then type a period. In this case, the title page of the encyclopedia lists two publishers in two locations.

> Kazdin, A. E. (Ed.). (2000). *Encyclopedia of psychology* (Vols. 1–8). Washington, DC: American Psychological Association. New York: Oxford University Press.

Doctoral Dissertation or Master's Thesis

Doctoral dissertation abstract
The *DAI (Dissertation Abstracts International)* volume and page number of the abstract are indicated, ending with a period.

> Esposito, J. (1987). Subjective factors and rumor transmission: A field investigation of the influence of anxiety, importance, and belief on rumormongering (Doctoral dissertation, Temple University, 1986). *Dissertation Abstracts International, 48,* 596B.

Unpublished doctoral dissertation
If a manuscript copy of the dissertation was used and the *DAI* number is not known, or if an abstract was not published in *DAI,* write "Unpublished doctoral dissertation" and give the university and location.

> Mettetal, G. W. (1982). The conversation of female friends at three ages: The importance of fantasy, gossip, and self-disclosure. Unpublished doctoral dissertation, University of Illinois, Urbana.

Master's thesis (outside the United States)
If a manuscript copy of a master's thesis was used and the *MAI (Master's Abstracts International)* number is not known, or if an abstract was not published in *MAI,* state "Unpublished master's thesis" and the college or university and location. In this case, observe that the title contains a British spelling ("organisational"), which a spelling checker might try to "correct."

> Hunt, E. (2000). *Correlates of uncertainty during organisational change.* Unpublished master's thesis, University of Queensland, St. Lucia, Queensland, Australia.

Unpublished Material

Technical report
The title of a technical report is italicized, followed by the report number in parentheses and the location and name of the organization that issued the report.

> LoSciuto, L. A., Aiken, L. S., & Ausetts, M. A. (1979). *Professional and paraprofessional drug abuse counselors: Three reports* (DHEW Publication No. 79-858). Rockville, MD: National Institute on Drug Abuse.

Unpublished manuscript
The title of an unpublished manuscript is indicated in italics, followed by "Unpublished manuscript" and the institution and its location.

> Burnham, J. R. (1966). *Experimenter bias and lesion labeling.* Unpublished manuscript, Purdue University, West Lafayette, IN.

Manuscript submitted for publication (but not yet accepted)
If a manuscript submitted for publication has not been formally accepted by the editor, then the name of the journal or book publisher to whom the manuscript was submitted should not be displayed. No matter whether the submitted manuscript is for a book, a chapter, or a journal article, the title of the manuscript is italicized.

> Mithalal, C. (2005). *Protocols of telephone therapy.* Manuscript submitted for publication.

Paper (unpublished) presented at a meeting
The month of the meeting is listed, the title of the paper is italicized, and the name of the sponsoring organization and the location of the meeting are indicated.

> Rajala, A. K., DeNicolis, J. L., Brecher, E. G., & Hantula, D. A (1995, May). *Investing in occupational safety: A utility analysis perspective.* Paper presented at the annual meeting of the Eastern Academy of Management, Ithaca, NY.

Poster presented at a meeting
Same as above.

> Freeman, M. A. (1995, August). *Demographic correlates of individualism and collectivism: A study of social values in Sri Lanka.* Poster presented at the annual meeting of the American Psychological Society, New York.

Audiovisual Media

Motion picture
After each primary contributor, the particular contribution is noted in parentheses, and "Motion picture" is inserted in brackets after the italicized title of the film. The country of origin (where the film was primarily made or released) and the motion picture studio are indicated.

> Zinneman, F. (Director), & Foreman, C. (Screenwriter). (1952). *High noon* [Motion picture]. United States: Universal Artists.

Television broadcast
The key here is simply to provide sufficient information to identify the broadcast as best you can, without leaving out any significant identifying detail.

> Doyle, W. (Producer). (2001, November 3). *An American insurrection* [Television broadcast]. New York: C-Span 2.

Music recording
The information in this example includes the composer's name, the date of copyright, the title of the piece, the recording artist, the title of the album

(Mahler–Bernstein), the medium of recording (CD, record, cassette, etc.), the location, and the record company.

> Mahler, G. (1991). Symphonie No. 8. [Recorded by L. Bernstein & Wiener Philharmoniker]. On *Mahler–Bernstein* [CD]. Hamburg, Germany: Deutsche Grammophon.

Electronic Sources

Some of the more common types of electronic references are illustrated below. However, because developments in the electronic media are in a constant state of flux, the APA regularly updates its electronic referencing Web site. If you have a specific reference that is not covered by the examples below, or a citation in text of electronic material that was not previously covered, go to the following APA Web site for information: http://www.apastyle.org/elecref.html

Abstract retrieved from PsycINFO
The article is cited in the usual way, but the fact that only the abstract (not the full text) was retrieved is indicated, followed by the date it was retrieved and the Web source.

> Morgeson, F. P., Seligman, M. E., Sternberg, R. J., Taylor, S. E., & Manning, C. M. (1999). Lessons learned from a life in psychological science: Implications for young scientists. *American Psychologist, 54,* 106–116. Abstract retrieved October 14, 1999, from PsycINFO database.

Full-text article retrieved from PsycARTICLES
Same as above, except for the omission of "Abstract" in the retrieval information.

> Egeth, H. E. (1993). What do we *not* know about eyewitness identification? *American Psychologist, 48,* 577–580. Retrieved January 14, 2002, from PsycARTICLES.

Same article retrieved electronically (another option)
Another suitable option when referencing articles retrieved electronically is to add "Electronic version" in brackets after the title, followed by a period, and then the full citation of the printed version.

> Egeth, H. E. (1993). What do we *not* know about eyewitness identification? [Electronic version]. *American Psychologist, 48,* 577–580.

Article in Internet-only journal
Whenever possible, the URL that links to the article is indicated. If the URL stretches to another line, then it should be broken after a slash or before a period, but do not insert a hyphen at the break.

> Lassiter, G. D., Munhall, P. J., Geers, A. L., Handley, I. M., & Weiland, P. E. (2001, November 1). Criminal confessions on videotape: Does

camera perspective bias their perceived veracity? *Current Research in
Social Psychology, 2,* 15–22. Retrieved November 2, 2001, from
www.uiowa.edu/~grpproc/crisp/crisp.7.1.htm

Information retrieved from Web site

The host or institutional provider of this information is listed, followed by the
date of the document or information (in parentheses, followed by a period),
and then the title of the document or information, and finally the retrieval
date and the URL.

American Psychological Association. (1999). Scholarships, grants and
funding opportunities. Retrieved October 14, 1999, www.apa.org/
students/grants.html

Proofing and Correcting

We now come to the final steps before you submit your paper: proofing and
correcting. Read the finished paper more than once. Ask yourself the following questions:

- Are there omissions?
- Are there misspellings?
- Are the numbers correct?
- Are the hyphenations correct?
- Do all the references cited in the body of the paper also appear in the
  references section?

The first time you read your final draft, the appeal of the neat, clean copy
may lead you to overlook errors. Put the paper aside for 24 hours, and then
read it carefully again. After you have corrected any errors, give the paper a
final look, checking to be sure all the pages are there and in order. If you ad-
hered to the guidelines in this manual, you should have the sense of a job well
done and should feel confident that the paper will receive the serious attention that a clear, consistent, and attractive manuscript deserves.

9

CRAFTING A POSTER AND A CONCISE REPORT

The poster is a visual display used to convey the nature and major findings of your research in the setting of a public forum. It is customary to provide interested viewers with a concise handout describing the research. The exercise of boiling down your research to its most pertinent components, without sacrificing vital details, will teach you the art of selecting critical information.

Posters and Handout Reports

It is becoming increasingly common for students doing empirical research not only to prepare a detailed written report of their findings, but also to present their results in poster form. Some posters may even be presented at conferences. This format has its own set of conventions and requirements, although they are not uniform. Instead, they depend on the parameters set forth by the organizers of each specific conference.

If you have an opportunity to attend a poster session, you can assess the visual impact of the various presentations. Which posters draw your eye? What is it about some posters that makes them more visually accessible than others? Poster presenters planning to do further research, or planning to write up their results for submission to a journal, find the feedback they obtain invaluable. If people are not drawn to the poster, however, there is no opportunity for feedback or discussion. Thus, it is important to create a poster that is visually inviting, and in this chapter, we provide guidelines to help you.

To supplement the information that is presented visually in the poster, a concise handout is also usually prepared. The report you prepared for class would be inappropriate as a handout. It is too costly to reproduce a lot of copies of a lengthy paper (the APA asks poster presenters to bring along 50 copies of the research report). Moreover, the paper you wrote for a course contains more information than anyone but your instructor will want to know. Thus, we also illustrate how to condense Jane Doe's detailed research report in Appendix A into a concise report for distribution.

Guidelines for the Poster

The way a poster session usually works is that you are asked to show up with your material in a large room or auditorium area, where you will see rows of display boards. Assuming you have not been assigned a particular board, it is first-come, first-served—so be sure to arrive early. Pushpins and Velcro hooks are usually available for attaching the pages to the display board. In advance of the meeting, some presenters, having arranged and pasted their pages on a cardboard poster, simply attach the whole poster to the display board. To be safe, it is a good idea to bring extra pushpins. You are not allowed to write, paint, or use paste on the display board, and you must have your display set up in the time allotted (10 minutes, for example), and then your display must be removed and the display board left neat and clean for the next set of presenters.

Exhibit 16 illustrates how guidelines for poster presentations may differ from one organization to another. The exhibit provides a comparison of poster elements distributed by the American Psychological Association (APA) and the American Association for the Advancement of Science (AAAS). Notice that, in virtually every respect, there is some difference. For example, the AAAS's poster board surface is two feet wider than the APA's; the larger the surface, the more information can be displayed. The APA guidelines recommend that an abstract of no more than 300 words be posted in the upper-left corner of the board surface, whereas the AAAS guidelines suggest that the sequence of information begin with the major conclusions.

It is impossible in this chapter to anticipate every special requirement you may encounter, but you can ensure that your poster will be suitable by finding out the requirements before you begin to design it. To help you get started, Exhibit 17 shows a compact template for a poster of only six 8½ × 11-inch pages and space for the title, author(s), and affiliation heading at the top. The material, allowing for some spacing between the pages and the heading, could be fitted onto a surface approximately 2 feet high and a little over 3 feet wide. The poster board surface furnished by the APA and the AAAS (Exhibit 16) allows the presenter more room to accommodate essential information, whereas Exhibit 17 illustrates how the research can be condensed when there is less space available. As you design your poster, remember that you are trying to draw attention to your study. You also want to chat with people who are interested in learning more about it, as well as to ferret out issues and ideas that can help you anticipate problems if you expect to submit the research to a journal or to continue doing research on this topic. One instructor told us that he cautioned students to be prepared for a cramped area with relatively poor lighting, a lot of distracting noise, and other sensory activity.

EXHIBIT 16   APA and AAAS poster design suggestions

Poster Element	APA	AAAS
Poster board surface	4' high, 6' wide	4' high, 8' wide
Legibility	At a 3' distance or more	At about a 5' distance
Sequence	Abstract (300 words or less) in upper-left corner, followed by ordered material (use numbers, letters, or arrows)	Conclusions, then supporting text, ending with brief summary
Title and author(s)	1" high, at least	2–3" high
Lettering of text	⅜" high, preferably boldface font, or hand-lettered with regular felt-tipped pen	24-point font, but can also use color as well as different sizes and proportions
Section headings	Label headings clearly	½–1" high subheadings
Tables and figures	Make them simple, clear, and easily visible	Graphics are preferable to tables
Handouts	50 copies, full paper	Abstract (number unspecified)

Here are three tips to keep in mind:

- ◆ Choose a font size that is big enough for tired, middle-aged viewers with failing eyesight to see from a distance.
- ◆ Keep the tables and figures simple, because people don't usually want to stand around and study them.
- ◆ Keeping it simple also means being selective in what you report, although it doesn't mean being evasive or misleading—only straightforward and concise.

Besides reviewing the specifics in Exhibit 16 and any information provided by the organizer of your poster session, here are further tips on how to format the poster:

- ◆ Use a typeface that is easy to read, such as Arial or Times New Roman, not a fancy one that has squiggles or loops.
- ◆ Make sure that your font size is visible at a distance, such as 24 points (one-quarter inch high; as recommended by the AAAS) or even 32 points.
- ◆ Don't overcomplicate tables or figures, and don't use jargon or exotic terms that are likely to be unfamiliar to your viewers.
- ◆ Use color for important highlights, but use it sparingly because you are reporting a scientific study, not creating a work of art.
- ◆ Make your figures and illustrations bold and self-explanatory, and be sure the details are easy to see.
- ◆ Organize and label the sequence of information in a way that leads the viewer through the poster, and leave some space to separate the parts of the poster.

Exhibit 18 shows sample text material for a poster using the six-page template in Exhibit 17 and Jane's research results. All that is missing are the

EXHIBIT 17   Template for a six-page poster

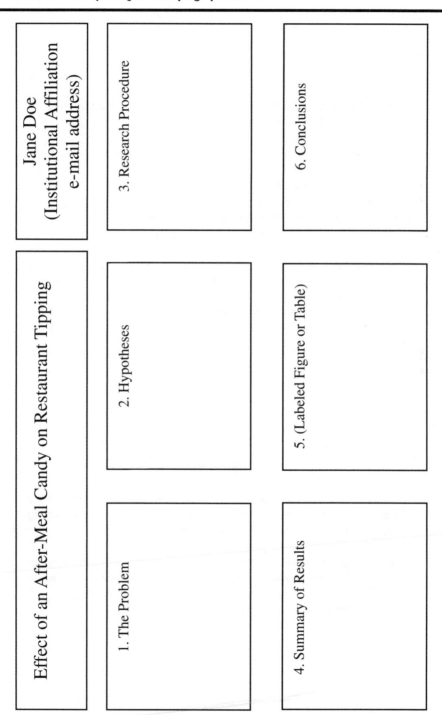

EXHIBIT 18 *Sample poster content*

---

1. The Problem

Empirical studies have found that the following techniques used by servers in restaurants can increase tipping:

- touching the recipient of the check on the palm of the hand for a fraction of a second
- giving customers sitting alone a large, open-mouth smile
- squatting to the eye level of customers
- telling customers one's first name during the initial visit
- drawing a happy face or writing "thank you" on the check.

All seem to have in common that servers are doing something that also increases customers' impressions of friendliness. In this study, another such technique was experimentally manipulated—offering customers an after-meal miniature chocolate candy.

---

2. Hypotheses

- It was predicted that merely offering customers an after-meal candy when presenting the check would increase tipping, and that offering them two pieces of candy would further increase tipping.

- Because people generally feel obligated to reciprocate when they receive an unexpected favor, it was predicted that creating an impression that the offer of a second candy reflected the server's generous impulse would produce the highest tips.

EXHIBIT 18   *Continued*

---

3. Research Procedure

The study involved 80 dining parties in an upscale restaurant in New Jersey, who were randomly assigned to the following conditions:

- *Control condition:* The server presented the check to customers at the end of the meal.

- *1-piece condition:* When presenting the check, the server had a basket of assorted miniature chocolates and offered each person 1 candy.

- *2-piece condition:* When presenting the check, the server offered each person 2 candies.

- *1 + 1 condition:* When presenting the check, the server offered 1 candy and said, "Oh, have another piece"—implying a generous afterthought.

---

4. Summary of Results

- As the Table of Results indicates, the pattern of tipping increased in the predicted direction, rising from the control to 1-piece to 2-piece to 1 + 1 conditions.

- A linear contrast was highly significant ($p < .0001$), and the 95% confidence interval for the effect size ranged from $r = .45$ to $.73$.

- The t tests comparing (a) the control and 2-piece conditions and (b) the control and 1 + 1 conditions were significant ($p < .0001$ one-tailed), both effect size $rs > .5$.

- The t test comparing the control and 1-piece conditions was not significant ($p = .17$ one-tailed, $r_{effect\ size} = .15$), but power was less than .5.

EXHIBIT 18   *Continued*

---

5. Table of Results

Mean Tip Percentage, Standard Deviation, and Sample Size

	Treatment condition			
Results	No candy	1 piece	2 pieces	1 + 1 pieces
M	18.95	19.59	21.62	22.99
SD	1.46	1.71	2.45	2.43
n	20	20	20	20

Note. Mean *(M)* value refers to average tip percentage in each condition. Tip percentage for each dining party was calculated by dividing the tip amount by the bill amount before taxes, then multiplying by 100. The standard deviation *(SD)* refers to the variability of $n = 20$ tip percentages around the mean value.

---

6. Conclusions

- Offering customers an after-meal candy can increase tip percentages, and two candies increase tips more than one candy. This finding is consistent with the idea that a token gift conveys friendliness, and that, in return, people give larger tips as a sign of their appreciation.

- Results in the 1 + 1 condition imply the role of reciprocity in increasing tips, in that people gave the largest tip percentages after being led to believe they were benefiting from the server's generous impulse.

- Further research is needed, however, to determine the generalizability of these findings to other servers, other types of restaurants, and other areas. Research is also needed to confirm the presumed mediational role of "friendliness" and "generosity" in the study.

title of Jane's poster, her name, and her institutional affiliation, all of which would be in boldface, mounted at the top of her poster. You can see that Jane's poster captures the highlights of her research study. If the sponsor requires that you begin with an abstract (as suggested by the APA), try to make it succinct, and let the rest of the poster lead viewers to the results and conclusions. Once you have created your poster, stand back a few feet and see if you can read it easily. You will also want to show it to your instructor, and to any others willing to give honest opinions about its readability and design.

Guidelines for the Concise Report

Because even the most interested viewers are unlikely to want to take extensive notes, have a written report they can take with them. The most economical approach would be to try to confine the vital information to two pages, so you can make copies of a one-page handout with information on both sides of the paper. Exhibit 19 illustrates such a handout based on Jane's research. If you compare it with her full report in Appendix A, you will detect how superfluous details have been excised and only the most essential information is included. Notice that there is space for Jane to provide her e-mail and institutional mailing address, should anyone wish to communicate with her about this research. Although the poster did not contain a list of references, there is an abbreviated list in the handout.

In preparing your brief report, you will want to consider the same criteria and guidelines that you consulted in developing the major sections of your full report. Your primary obligation is to give people a clear, precise understanding of how the research was done, what you found, and what you concluded. Here are three helpful guidelines:

- Try to anticipate people's questions. For example, think about the comments your instructor wrote on your paper.
- Tell people enough.
- At the very least, report (a) group means, (b) sample sizes, and (c) measurement error, because these minimal raw ingredients are needed for any reanalysis of the results.

Finally, bring along a manila envelope, labeled HANDOUTS. Slip 50 or more copies of your report inside, and attach it to the poster board, making your research readily available to any interested poster viewers.

EXHIBIT 19 *Sample brief report for distribution*

Effect of an After-Meal Candy on Restaurant Tipping

Jane Doe[*]
(Institutional affiliation and/or mailing address for correspondence)
(e-mail address)

*This brief report is based on a poster of the same title, which was presented at
(name of meeting, date of presentation, location of meeting).*

Background and Hypotheses

More than 1 million people in the United States work as waiters and waitresses. Although they usually receive wages from their employers, the major source of income for servers comes in the form of tips from customers. Research studies have demonstrated techniques for encouraging tipping, including (a) touching customers twice on the palm of the hand for a fraction of a second (Hornik, 1992); (b) giving customers sitting alone a large, open-mouth smile (Tidd & Lockard, 1978); (c) squatting to the eye level of customers (Lynn & Mynier, 1993); (d) introducing oneself by one's first name at the initial visit (Garrity & Degelman, 1990); and (e) writing "thank you" or drawing a happy face on the check (Rind & Bordia, 1995, 1996).

These techniques seem to have in common that the servers are doing something that may also increase customers' impressions of friendliness. In this study, another technique along this line was experimentally evaluated, guided by the following three hypotheses:
1. When presenting the check, merely offering customers an after-meal candy will increase tipping.
2. On the assumption this effect is cumulative, offering two pieces of candy will further increase tipping.
3. Because people generally feel obligated to reciprocate when they receive a favor (cf. Regan, 1971), creating the impression that the offer of a second candy is a favor reflecting the server's own generous impulse will produce the largest tipping percentage.

Method

A total of 80 dining parties in an upscale Italian-American restaurant in New Jersey were assigned at random to one of four conditions, 20 units per condition. In the *control condition,* the server simply presented the check to the customers at the end of the meal. In the three other conditions, the server was given a basket of miniature chocolates to take with her when presenting the check: In the *1-piece condition*, she offered each person in the dining party 1 candy of his or her choice. In the *2-piece condition,* she offered each person 2 candies. In the *1 + 1 condition,* she offered a candy and then said, "Oh, have another piece," to create the impression of a generous afterthought.

Results

The dependent measure was defined as the tip percentage—that is, the tip amount divided by the amount of the bill before taxes, which was then multiplied by 100. Based on the hypotheses, the overall prediction was that the average tip percentage in the four groups would increase from control to 1-piece to 2-piece to 1 + 1 conditions.

---

[*] I thank Dr. Bruce Rind for providing me with valuable guidance throughout this research project, and also thank the owner of the restaurant and the server for making it possible for me to carry out this research.

EXHIBIT 19   Continued

Results indicated that the pattern of tip percentages was exactly as predicted. The average value was (a) 18.95% ($SD = 1.46$) in the control, (b) 19.59% ($SD = 1.71$) in the 1-piece condition, (c) 21.62% ($SD = 2.45$) in the 2-piece condition, and (d) 22.99% ($SD = 2.43$) in the 1 + 1 condition. A linear contrast (with lambda weights of -3, -1, +1, +3, respectively) was highly significant and the effect size large, $F(1, 76) = 44.97$, $p < .0001$, $r_{effect\ size} = .61$ (95% confidence interval ranged from $r_{effect\ size} = .45$ to .73).

Independent t tests comparing the control and the other three conditions, using $MSE = 4.45$ and $df = 76$, were significant only for the (a) control vs. 2-piece comparison ($t = 3.99$, $p < .0001$, $r_{effect\ size} = .54$) and (b) control vs. 1 + 1 comparison ($t = 6.05$, $p < .0001$, $r_{effect\ size} = .61$). The control vs. 1-piece comparison, with statistical power less than .5, resulted in $t = .95$, $p = .17$ one-tailed, $r_{effect\ size} = .15$.

Conclusions

The pattern of tip percentages (and the linear contrast) is consistent with the idea that offering a token gift of candy to customers can increase tip percentages, and offering two candies is better than offering one candy. The theoretical explanation may be that offering people a token gift conveys a sense of friendliness, in return for which they respond amiably by rewarding the server with a larger tip. Results in the 1 + 1 condition implied the role of reciprocity, as customers responded with the largest tips when they were led to believe they were recipients of the server's personal generosity.

Because only one waitress participated in this study, research is needed to establish the generalizability of the findings to male servers as well as to other female servers, other types of restaurants, and other areas. Further research is also needed to confirm the presumed role of "friendliness" and "generosity."

References

Garrity, K., & Degelman, D. (1990). Effect of server introduction on restaurant tipping. *Journal of Applied Social Psychology, 20,* 168-172.

Hornik, J. (1992). Tactile stimulation and consumer response. *Journal of Consumer Research, 19,* 449-458.

Lynn, M., & Mynier, K. (1993). Effect of server posture on restaurant tipping. *Journal of Applied Social Psychology, 23,* 678-685.

Regan, D. T. (1971). Effects of a favor and liking on compliance. *Journal of Experimental Social Psychology, 7,* 627-639.

Rind, B., & Bordia, P. (1995). Effect of server's "thank you" and personalization on restaurant tipping. *Journal of Applied Social Psychology, 25,* 745-751.

Rind, B., & Bordia, P. (1996). Effect on restaurant tipping of male and female servers drawing a happy, smiling face on the backs of customers' checks. *Journal of Applied Social Psychology, 26,* 218-225.

Tidd, K., & Lockard, J. (1978). Monetary significance of the affiliative smile: A case for reciprocal altruism. *Bulletin of the Psychometric Society, 11,* 344-346.

A

JANE DOE'S
RESEARCH REPORT

Pages are numbered consecutively, beginning with the title page, and contain a short heading of two or three words from the title.

Restaurant Tipping   1

Effect of an After-Meal Candy on Restaurant Tipping:

An Experimental Study in a Naturalistic Setting

The title is double-spaced in uppercase and lowercase letters and centered between the left and right margins.

The student's name and e-mail address are centered, two double-spaced lines below the title.

Jane Doe

(e-mail address or other contact information)

Psych 333

Instructor: Prof. Bruce Rind

(Date the Research Report Is Submitted)

The course number, the instructor's name, and the date the paper is submitted are double-spaced.

The abstract begins on a new page.

Restaurant Tipping   2

Abstract

The abstract is not indented.

Previous research has shown that waiters and waitresses (i.e., servers) can increase their tips by using a variety of techniques that generally involve creating an impression of friendliness. This study examined another technique that was hypothesized to enhance customers' favorable impressions of the server and, in turn, increase the size of the tip. The server in this study was provided with a basket of miniature chocolate candies, which she was instructed to bring with her when presenting the check in three experimental conditions. In the "1-piece condition," the server offered each customer in the dining party one candy of his or her choice. In the "2-piece condition," the server offered each person two candies, on the premise that this gesture would further underscore the server's friendliness. In the "1+1 condition," she offered one candy and said, "Oh, have another piece"; this procedure was intended to emphasize not only her friendliness but also her personal generosity (consistent with reciprocity theory). In the control condition, the server presented the check without any candy offer. Although the tip percentage in the control condition differed significantly only from that in the 2-piece and 1+1 conditions, there was, as hypothesized, increased tipping from control group to 1-piece to 2-piece to 1+1 condition; the linear contrast was statistically significant and the effect size substantial. Statistical power considerations and ideas for further investigation are discussed.

For conciseness, digits are used for all numbers in the abstract, except those that begin a sentence.

Briefly, the abstract tells why the research was done, what was hypothesized, what the results were, and what else appears in the discussion section.

Use a 12-point typeface, preferably Times New Roman or Courier.

The first line of every paragraph in the text is indented five to seven spaces.

The opening paragraph sets the stage in an inviting way and explains the importance of the research.

The statistical symbol for a percentage (%) is used only when it is preceded by a number.

Effect of an After-Meal Candy on Restaurant Tipping:

An Experimental Study in a Naturalistic Setting

More than 1 million people in the United States work as waiters or waitresses who serve in restaurants (Department of Commerce, 1990, p. 391). Although they are generally paid for their service by their employers, the major source of income for servers is usually tips from customers (Lynn & Mynier, 1993; Schmidt, 1985). Because tips are so important to the livelihood of most servers, knowledge about factors that affect customers' tipping behavior is valuable. A growing number of studies have examined factors hypothesized to affect tipping. This research has shown that servers can increase their tipping percentages by a variety of techniques (Lynn, 1996).

Some of these techniques involve direct interpersonal action on the part of the server, such as smiling at or touching the customer. For example, Hornik (1992) had three waitresses at two restaurants either not touch their customers, touch them for half a second on the shoulder, or touch them twice on the palm of the hand for half a second each time. Tips increased from 12% to 14% to 17% in the three conditions, respectively. Tidd and Lockard (1978) had a waitress give customers sitting alone a large, open-mouth smile or a small, closed-mouth smile. Customers in the former condition tipped on average more than twice as much as in the latter condition. In a similar vein, Lynn and Mynier (1993) instructed servers either to squat to the eye level of their customers or stand erect during the initial visit to the table; the squatting increased tips. Garrity and Degelman (1990) reported that a server earned higher tips when introducing herself by her first name during her initial visit (23% average tip) than when she did not introduce herself (15% average tip).

Other effective techniques employed an indirect stimulus to encourage tipping. For example, Rind and Bordia (1996) had servers either draw or not draw

The text begins on a new page and opens with a repetition of the title.

An ampersand (&) appears in parentheses where "and" is used otherwise.

Although the left margin is even, the right margin is ragged.

Citations buttress the introduction.

On all four sides, leave a margin of at least 1 inch, providing room for the reader's comments.

Restaurant Tipping 4

a happy face on the backs of customers' checks before delivering them. The happy face increased tips for the female server but did not increase tips for the male server (for whom this practice may have been regarded as "gender-inappropriate" by customers). Rind and Bordia (1995) also found that writing "thank you" on the backs of checks resulted in an increase in tips from 16% to 18%. Finally, McCall and Belmont (1995) had servers present checks either on a tray with credit card emblems on it or on a tray with no emblems and found that tipping percentages were higher in the former condition.

These techniques, except for the last one, have in common that the servers were doing something that might increase the customers' impressions of friendliness. Another such technique was experimentally examined in the present study. When presenting the check to the dining party, the server sometimes also presented a gift of assorted candies. Three hypotheses were investigated. First, on the assumption that the gift would be perceived by customers as a gesture of friendliness, it was predicted that the presentation of the gift would have the effect of stimulating tipping, in comparison with a no-gift control group. On the assumption that this effect is cumulative (i.e., up to a certain point), the second hypothesis was that an offer of more candies would stimulate tipping even more. The third hypothesis was that when customers were under the impression that the offer of a gift also reflected the server's generosity (i.e., as opposed to the restaurant's protocol), there would be a further increase in tipping. This third hypothesis was derived from research on reciprocity, which found that individuals feel especially obligated to return a favor to the person responsible for the favor (Regan, 1971).

Method

Participants

Eighty dining parties eating dinner at an upscale Italian-American restaurant located in central New Jersey served as participants. The total number of customers in the dining parties was 293, with a mean of 3.67 customers per dining party (SD = 1.97). The size of the dining parties ranged from 2 to 12.

Procedure

A female server, who also served as the experimental accomplice, was provided with a small wicker basket that was filled with Hershey Assorted Miniature chocolates. The candies were of four types: (a) dark chocolate bars, (b) milk chocolate bars, (c) rice-and-chocolate bars, and (d) peanut-butter-and-chocolate bars. The server was also given a stack of index cards, each of which contained an instruction telling her to do one of four things when presenting the check. In the control condition, she was instructed to present the check as usual without any candy offer. In the three experimental conditions, she was instructed to bring along the basket of candy when presenting the check.

In one experimental condition, the server was instructed to offer each customer in the dining party one piece of candy of his or her choice (the "1-piece condition"). In a second experimental condition, she was instructed to offer each customer in the party two pieces of candy (the "2-piece condition"). In the third experimental condition, she was instructed to offer one candy and then say, "Oh, have another piece," as if the offer of a second piece were a generous afterthought (the "1+1 condition"); this treatment was intended to emphasize to customers the server's (as opposed to the restaurant's) generosity.

The cards were thoroughly shuffled to ensure that the order of the four types of instructions was random. When it was time to present the check, the server reached into her apron pocket and randomly chose a card. The server was instructed to thank the dining party after their selection of candies, and then to leave the table immediately to avoid any nonessential interaction with the party. After the dining party had left the restaurant, the server recorded (on the same card

The list is lettered for clarity.

Double quotation marks are used here to indicate that the term is an invented expression, but quotation marks are not used again when the expression is repeated later.

Double quotation marks here because this was the verbatim statement by the server.

Restaurant Tipping   6

used to determine the dining party's treatment condition) the amount of the tip left by the party, the amount of the bill before taxes, and the party size.

Results

All the data collected and a description of my calculations appear in the appendix of this report, beginning with a table showing the tip percentages in each condition. The tip percentage is defined as the tip amount divided by the bill amount before taxes; the result was then multiplied by 100 to yield a percentage. The summary results are given in Table 1, which shows average tip percentages in the four conditions—that is, the arithmetic means (M) of the columns of values shown in the appendix table. As Table 1 shows, there was an increase, as predicted, in the mean tip percentage from the control (no candy) to the 1-piece condition, to the 2-piece condition, and to the 1+1 condition. The omnibus F shown in Table 2 was of little relevance to this prediction, with $F(3, 76) = 15.51$, $p = 5.8^{-8}$, as the same F would have been obtained had the conditions been in another order. However, the purpose of the omnibus F was (a) to obtain a more stable value of the mean square error required in the denominator of my t tests, and (b) to show how the sum of squares of a contrast F designed to test the prediction noted above was carved out of the between-groups sum of squares.

There were three hypotheses and thus three specific predictions. The first prediction was that tipping would be greater in the 1-piece condition than in the control condition. As mentioned above, Table 1 shows the direction of these two group means to be consistent with this prediction. A t test comparing the two conditions was not statistically significant, however, with $t(76) = .95$, $p = .17$ one-tailed. The corresponding effect size correlation, calculated from the t statistic, was $r_{\text{effect size}} = .15$, and the 95% confidence interval ranged from $r_{\text{effect size}} = -.17$ to .44, which left open the possibility of a small effect in the opposite direction in the interval containing the population effect size.

The results section follows the method section without a page break.

Statistical symbol for the mean.

The student mentions Table 1.

The student interprets the results in Table 1.

Degrees of freedom are 3 for the numerator and 76 for the denominator of this F statistic.

Degrees of freedom are 76 for this t test, and the p value is denoted as one-tailed.

Restaurant Tipping   7

On the assumption that the effect of the server's gift giving on subsequent tipping would be cumulative, the second prediction was that the tipping would be still greater in the 2-piece than in the control condition. The means in Table 1 are again consistent with the hypothesis, and in this case, the difference between the control condition and the 2-piece condition was significant, with $t(76) = 3.99$, $p = 7.5^{-5}$ one-tailed. The effect size correlation associated with this t was $r_{effect size} = .54$, and the 95% confidence interval ranged from .28 to .73. Thus, there is a 95% probability that this range of values will contain the population value of the effect size r reflecting membership in the control versus the 2-piece condition as a predictor of the tip percentage.

The third prediction, which was derived from reciprocity research, was that creating the impression that the server was generous (the 1+1 condition) would result in a further increase in tipping. The t test comparing the 1+1 and control conditions was significant, with $t(76) = 6.05$, $p = 2.5^{-8}$ one-tailed, and the associated $r_{effect size} = .70$; the 95% confidence interval of the effect size r ranged from .50 to .83.

Finally, to provide a focused evaluation of the increase in tipping from control to 1-piece to 2-piece to 1+1 conditions, a linear contrast was computed. In contrast analysis, the prediction of interest is represented by fixed weights (called *lambda weights*) that must sum to zero. I chose lambda weights of -3, -1, +1, +3 to represent the predicted linear increase from control to 1-piece to 2-piece to 1+1 groups. All of the calculations are shown in the appendix of this report. The results are summarized in Table 2. As this table shows, the linear contrast F, with 1 and 76 degrees of freedom, was 44.97, with $p = 3.1^{-9}$ and the effect size $r = .61$; the 95% confidence interval ranged from $r_{effect size} = .45$ to .73.

Discussion

Prior to implementing this research, it was hypothesized that offering a favor in the form of chocolate candies would stimulate tipping, and that the more

---

Confidence interval of the effect size is also reported.

Each prediction is reiterated, and the relevant finding is reported.

A technical term ("lambda weights") is defined.

Symbol for "r" is in italics, but the subscript term ("effect size") is not.

Many statisticians report the actual descriptive level of significance because it is more precise than "$p < .01$."

The student mentions that the raw data and calculations are in the appendix at the end of this paper.

The discussion follows the results section without a page break.

The discussion begins with a statement of the predictions and the results.

Restaurant Tipping   8

candy offered, the greater would be the tip, with the largest tip percentage predicted in the condition in which the server was also meant to be perceived as personally responsible for the gift. Although the four condition means are consistent with these hypotheses, and the linear contrast was consistent with the hypothesized monotonic increase in tipping, the t test comparing the control and 1-piece conditions was not statistically significant. From my reading of Cohen (1992), it was evident that the power of the t test comparing the control and 1-piece conditions was much lower than the recommended level of .80.

The APA manual emphasizes the importance of statistical power in null hypothesis significance testing, particularly when negative results are reported.

There are many ways to improve statistical power, which include administering stronger treatments and increasing sample sizes. At this point, I am unable to think of ways of strengthening the treatments I used, and even had I been able to anticipate the need for larger samples, I was limited by time: The research had to be conducted, analyzed, and reported by the end of this semester. If there is an opportunity to replicate this study, another way to improve statistical power would be to obtain an overall p value based on the meta-analytic combination of the two studies, assuming they have similar results.

Clearly, further research is also needed to replicate the relationships in this investigation, particularly to investigate the reliability of the present findings and the separate and interacting roles of reciprocity and perceptions of friendliness. There is a need as well to verify the roles of "friendliness" and "generosity" implicit in my hypotheses. Finally, additional research is needed to study the generalizability of the findings to male servers and other female servers, other types of restaurants (e.g., midscale), other regions of the country, and other types of gifts. At this point, however, I definitely plan to try out the 1+1 chocolates strategy when I return to my summer job as a waitress on Cape Cod.

The discussion concludes by noting the limitations of the study and ideas for further investigation.

Publication in which the author is also the publisher.

The references begin on a new page.

Restaurant Tipping   9

References

American Psychological Association. (2001). *Publication manual of the American Psychological Association* (5th ed.). Washington, DC: Author.

Cohen, J. (1992). A power primer. *Psychological Bulletin, 112,* 155-159.

Department of Commerce. (1990). *Statistical abstracts of the United States.* Washington, DC: Author.

Garrity, K., & Degelman, D. (1990). Effect of server introduction on restaurant tipping. *Journal of Applied Social Psychology, 20,* 168-172.

Hornik, J. (1992). Tactile stimulation and consumer response. *Journal of Consumer Research, 19,* 449-458.

Lynn, M. (1996). Seven ways to increase servers' tips. *Cornell Hotel and Restaurant Administration Quarterly, 37*(3), 24-29.

Lynn, M., & Mynier, K. (1993). Effect of server posture on restaurant tipping. *Journal of Applied Social Psychology, 23,* 678-685.

McCall, M., & Belmont, H. J. (1995). *Credit card insignia and tipping: Evidence for an associative link.* Unpublished manuscript, Ithaca College.

Regan, D. T. (1971). Effects of a favor and liking on compliance. *Journal of Experimental Social Psychology, 7,* 627-639.

Rind, B., & Bordia, P. (1995). Effect of server's "thank you" and personalization on restaurant tipping. *Journal of Applied Social Psychology, 25,* 745-751.

Rind, B., & Bordia, P. (1996). Effect on restaurant tipping of male and female servers drawing a happy, smiling face on the backs of customers' checks. *Journal of Applied Social Psychology, 26,* 218-225.

Schmidt, D. G. (1985). Tips: The mainstay of hotel workers' pay. *Monthly Labor Review, 108,* 50-61.

Tidd, K., & Lockard, J. (1978). Monetary significance of the affiliative smile: A case for reciprocal altruism. *Bulletin of the Psychometric Society, 11,* 344-346.

Government report.

Journal article with two authors.

One-author entries precede multiple-author entries beginning with the same surname.

References with the same authors in the same order are arranged by year of publication.

Capitalize proper nouns in the title.

Journal titles and volume numbers are in italics.

Unpublished manuscript.

Journal article with one author.

Capitalize the first word of the title and the subtitle.

References are double-spaced in a hanging-indent format, with five-to-seven-space indent.

Table number and title (which is in italics) are flush left.

Where means are reported, an associated measure of variability is also reported.

Table notes are placed below the table, and in this case, the note clearly explains what appears in the table.

Row and column headings are telegraphic.

The word "Note" is italicized and followed by a period.

Tables are placed after the references, each table on its own separate page.

Restaurant Tipping   10

Table 1

Mean Tip Percentage, Standard Deviation, and Sample Size

	Treatment condition			
Results	No candy	1 piece	2 pieces	1+1 pieces
M	18.95	19.59	21.62	22.99
SD	1.46	1.71	2.45	2.43
n	20	20	20	20

Note. The mean *(M)* value denotes the average tip percentage in the particular condition; I calculated the tip percentage for each dining party by dividing the tip amount by the bill amount before taxes, and then multiplying by 100. The standard deviation *(SD)* refers to the variability of $n = 20$ tip percentages around the mean value.

Table 2 begins
on a new page.

Table 2

Analysis of Variance with Linear Contrast

Source	SS	df	MS	F	$r_{effect\ size}$
Between groups	207.06	3	69.02	15.51*	--
Linear contrast	200.12	1	200.12	44.97*	.61
Noncontrast	6.94	2	3.47	0.78	--
Within error	338.22	76	(4.45)		

Note. The value enclosed in parentheses represents mean square error. No effect size indicator is represented for the two *F* tests with numerator *df* > 1, as "multiple degree-of-freedom indicators tend to be less useful than effect indicators that decompose multiple degree-of-freedom tests into meaningful one degree-of-freedom effects" (American Psychological Association, 2001, p. 26).

*p < .0001

Because the linear contrast and noncontrast sums of squares were carved out of the between-groups sum of squares, the carved-out sources are slightly indented to represent this fact.

The mean square error (MSE) is enclosed in parentheses.

The page number of the quoted statement is indicated.

The APA style is to use asterisks or daggers to identify probability levels in tables.

The APA style is to round values to two decimal places to make the values read more easily in tables that contain a lot of information.

The appendix begins on a new page and is the final section of the report.

Appendix

The data shown below are tip percentages, calculated by multiplying the tip

amount by the bill amount before taxes, and then multiplying this product by 100:

	No candy	1 piece	2 pieces	1+1 piece
	18.92	18.87	22.78	17.38
	18.43	20.49	15.81	23.38
	18.67	17.54	19.16	25.05
	18.27	19.35	19.01	21.83
	18.92	20.65	21.60	24.43
	17.84	19.17	18.45	21.11
	19.57	19.73	23.41	25.09
	19.12	17.88	21.37	24.35
	18.67	21.00	22.01	25.37
	22.94	22.33	20.65	21.87
	19.26	19.75	20.92	23.87
	19.49	20.79	26.17	22.62
	19.12	20.52	23.31	26.73
	15.90	22.66	23.85	21.81
	19.29	18.60	22.30	23.60
	19.12	18.60	21.34	23.06
	21.70	20.07	18.89	24.05
	16.72	14.64	23.47	16.72
	17.75	19.01	25.69	22.43
	19.35	20.08	22.12	25.08
M	18.9525	19.5865	21.6155	22.9915
S	1.4948	1.7525	2.5092	2.4898
σ	1.4570	1.7081	2.4457	2.4268

It is not necessary to type the appendix, but it is important to provide the instructor with the raw data and sufficient details to explain how you computed the results, if you did so on a handheld calculator.

The pooled error term is the average of the squared S values above, or

$S^2_{pooled} = 4.4502$. The sum of squares between groups is the sum of the squared

weighted deviations between the four group means and the grand mean

(20.7865), as calculated below:

$$SS_{between} = \sum \left[n_k \left(M_k - M_G \right)^2 \right]$$
$$= 20\left(18.9525-20.7865\right)^2 + 20\left(19.5865-20.7865\right)^2$$
$$+ 20\left(21.6155-20.7865\right)^2 + 20\left(21.9915-20.7865\right)^2$$
$$= 207.0564$$

Formulas can be written in by hand, if that is easier.

The calculations are reported in a way that walks the reader through the logical sequence used, clearly explaining how the summary results in the research report were obtained.

The omnibus F in Table 2 was calculated as follows:

$$F(3,76) = \frac{SS_{between} / (k-1)}{S^2_{pooled}} = \frac{207.0564 / 3}{4.4502} = 15.5091$$

Independent t tests, using the pooled error term above and $df = N - k$ (corresponding to this error term), compared the 1-piece vs. control, the 2-piece vs. control, and the 1+1 piece vs. control, all using the following formula:

$$t = \frac{M_1 - M_2}{\sqrt{\left(\frac{1}{n_1} + \frac{1}{n_2}\right)S^2_{pooled}}}, \text{ and } r_{effect\,size} = \sqrt{\frac{t^2}{t^2 + df}}$$

with df for the effect size $r = n_1 + n_2 - 2$. Thus, for the 1-piece vs. control comparison, the results were:

$$t = \frac{19.5865 - 18.9525}{\sqrt{\left(\frac{1}{20} + \frac{1}{20}\right)4.4502}} = 0.9504, \text{ and } r_{effect\,size} = \sqrt{\frac{(.9504)^2}{(.9504)^2 + 38}} = .1524$$

The results, although rounded to two decimal places in the text, are not rounded in the calculations.

Contrast weights for the hypothesized linear increase in tipping from control to 1-piece to 2-piece to 1+1 conditions were -3, -1, +1, +3, which, when correlated with the four group means, yielded $r_{alerting} = .9831$. Squaring this value indicated the proportion of $SS_{between}$ accounting for the contrast weights. Multiplying the squared alerting r (.9665) by $SS_{between}$ (207.0564) resulted in the contrast sum of squares in Table 2. The effect size r for the contrast was calculated as follows:

$$r_{effect\,size} = \sqrt{\frac{F_{contrast}}{F_{contrast} + F_{noncontrast}\left(df_{noncontrast}\right) + df_{within}}}$$

$$= \sqrt{\frac{44.9688}{44.9688 + 0.7793(2) + 76}} = .6058$$

The student explains the calculations, indicating her depth of understanding to the instructor.

B

JOHN SMITH'S
REVIEW PAPER

The title is double-spaced in uppercase and lowercase letters and centered between the left and right margins.

Perspectives on Intelligence   1

Two Major Perspectives on Human Intelligence

Pages are numbered consecutively, beginning with the title page, and contain a short heading of two or more words from the title.

The student's name and e-mail address are centered, two double-spaced lines below the title.

John Smith

(e-mail address or other contact information)

Psych 222

Instructor: Prof. Anne Skleder

(Date the Paper Is Submitted)

The course number, the instructor's name, and the date the paper is submitted are double-spaced.

The abstract begins on a new page.

The abstract is not indented.

Abstract

Two perspectives on the nature of human intelligence are compared. Traditionally, in psychology, intelligence has been viewed as *g*-centric, meaning that a general trait (labeled *g*) is thought to be a component of every valid measure of human intelligence. Contrasting with this classic idea is what I describe as the *multiplex view,* which is the more recently developed position arguing that there are different kinds of intelligence that do not necessarily have a common psychometric core. The focal point of this discussion is Howard Gardner's theory of multiple intelligences. Criticisms of multiplex theories of intelligence are examined. The paper concludes with a broad overview of the direction of work in this area.

The term *g* is italicized.

The abstract tells why the paper was written and, very briefly, what the paper argues or explains in the context of its purpose.

The first line of every paragraph in the text is indented five to seven spaces.

Defined scientific and technical terms are italicized.

First-level headings are centered, whereas second-level headings are flush left and in italics.

Perspectives on Intelligence   3

The text begins on a new page and opens by repeating the title.

Although the left margin is even, the right margin is ragged.

All the major sections of the text follow each other without a break.

Two Major Perspectives on Human Intelligence

People use the word *intelligence* and its various synonyms in many different ways to refer to distinct aptitudes. Some individuals are called *book smart,* a term meaning that they are strong in verbal or mathematical aptitudes. Others are referred to as *street smart,* a term implying that they are intellectually shrewd in the ways of the world. Still others are said to have *business savvy* or *political sense* or the ability to *read people like a book,* phrases meaning that their skills involve interpersonal aptitude that may not be directly measured by standard tests of intelligence. This paper examines the nature of human intelligence from two major perspectives. One position is frequently characterized as the *g-centric view* because it reflects the psychometric assumption of a general trait *(g)* that is presumed to be at the core of human intelligence. The second major position, which is more recent, is characterized here as the *multiplex view* because it reflects the assumption of multiple intelligences housed within the same culture (but not necessarily in any single individual within the culture). I begin by elaborating on the distinction between these two perspectives and then focus on one prominent example of the multiplex view, the work of Howard Gardner (1983, 1985). Two main criticisms of multiplex theories are examined, and the paper concludes with an overview of what I understand to be the direction of work in this area.

Two General Conceptions of Intelligence

Evolution of the Traditional View

In a recent article, historian of psychology Ludy T. Benjamin, Jr. (2004) noted that the earliest measures of intelligence included head size, reaction time, and sensory abilities. In his words:

Head size was used as a measure of brain size, reaction time was thought to be a measure of the speed of information processing, and because the senses were judged to be so critical in the acquisition of information, it was assumed that they were important in differentiating levels of intelligence. These

A quotation of 40 or more words is set off from the body of the text by means of indented margins, and quotation marks are omitted.

Perspectives on Intelligence   4

anthropometric intelligence tests would be found to be unrelated to school

performance once the correlation coefficient was invented, and they would be

replaced by the intelligence tests developed by Alfred Binet. (p. 12)

Following the development of Binet's paper-and-pencil measures and later

developments in the field of statistics, research for much of the 20th century

focused on the existence of a general overriding trait of intelligence, usually

measured by short-answer tests of mathematical and linguistic skills. Influenced

by the theoretical and psychometric contributions of Charles Spearman (1927),

who regarded intelligence as a general characteristic, psychological and

educational researchers in the intelligence test movement accepted as valid the g-

centric (or g-centered) idea of intelligence. A number of leading psychometricians,

such as Arthur Jensen (1969), further argued that differences in g can be attributed

largely to heritability (genetic factors) as opposed to environmental or cultural

influences, a position that has been contested in psychology and education.

Regarding the essential idea of a general characteristic of intelligence, child

development researchers inspired by the theoretical and empirical work of Jean

Piaget also argued for the idea of general structures of the mind (Siegler &

Richards, 1982). These structures, they asserted, develop in a similar way in all

children. In the biological area, some investigators have attempted to

operationalize g by measuring the speed of neural transmission (Reed & Jensen,

1992) or by using measures of hemispheric localization (Levy, 1974). In the

1990s, a controversial reanalysis of IQ test data by Herrnstein and Murray (1994),

in a book entitled *The Bell Curve,* ignited a spirited debate about the presumed

role of g in the lives of individuals and in the larger social order. Thus, although

the traditional view of intelligence has been periodically challenged, many noted

psychologists consider fundamental the idea that standard IQ tests provide

numbers that allow us to distinguish "bright" people from the "not-so-bright" in

terms of accrued knowledge or potential for learning.

The list is lettered for clarity.

In sum, whether psychologists and educators mean by *intelligence* (a) the ability to adapt to the environment, (b) the ability to deal with symbols or abstractions, or (c) the ability to learn, many noted researchers assume that a core ingredient in these aptitudes is the factor known as *g* (Gilbert, 1971). Recently, Frey and Detterman (2004) asserted that the Scholastic Assessment Test (SAT) is basically a surrogate measure of general intelligence *(g)* and can be used to predict cognitive functioning when other indicators of general intelligence are unavailable. In one study, these researchers extracted a measure of *g* from the Armed Services Vocational Aptitude Battery and observed the correlation with SAT scores to be $r = .82$ (.86 corrected for nonlinearity) in a sample of 917 subjects aged 14 to 21 from a national probability data set. In a second study, they used a sample of 104 undergraduate students, recruited through the psychology subject pool, to investigate the relationship between SAT scores and scores on the Raven's Progressive Matrices (a test of nonverbal reasoning skills) and found $r = .483$ (.72 corrected for restricted range). Frey and Detterman also provided equations for estimating IQ from SAT scores, whether the SAT was taken before or after the 1994 recentering of scores.

Abbreviations are spelled out first.

One early criticism of the traditional *g*-centered view of intelligence was expressed by L. L. Thurstone (1938) and his coworkers. On the basis of the psychometric studies they conducted with large numbers of participants, Thurstone and Thurstone (1941) concluded that there are distinct aptitudes, which they called "primary mental abilities," including verbal comprehension, word fluency, numerical ability, and spatial relations. More recently, Sternberg and Berg (1986) reported that a panel of experts had embraced diverse, and ostensibly divergent, factors in what they theoretically associated with intelligence. Although controversy continues to surround the meaning of intelligence as well as its relation to real-world skills, a task force of the American Psychological Association (APA) nevertheless was able to agree on a list of "knowns" about intelligence (Neisser, Boodoo, Bouchard, Boykin, Brody, Ceci, et al., 1996).

The first full citation of a work lists up to six authors.

Perspectives on Intelligence   6

Evolution of the Multiplex View

In his classic book, J. P. Guilford (1967) developed the theory that ordinary intelligence encompasses multiple aptitudes and, in turn, raised the possibility that there are over a hundred different ways in which individuals can excel intellectually. Moving the idea of multiple abilities in still another direction, Robert Sternberg (1990)—one of the coauthors of the APA report by Neisser et al. (1996)—also argued that the nature of the information processing measured by standard IQ tests is actually quite different from that involved in certain kinds of complex reasoning in everyday life. By way of illustration, Ceci and Liker (1986) reported that skill in handicapping racehorses could not be predicted from handicappers' performance on the Wechsler Adult Intelligence Scale. Sternberg, Wagner, Williams, and Horvath (1995) concluded that "even the most charitable estimates of the relation between intelligence test scores and real-world criteria such as job performance indicate that approximately three-fourths of the variance in real-world performance is not accounted for by intelligence test performance" (p. 912). Although Rosenthal (1990) showed, in another context, that identifying a predictor variable that can account for 25% of variance is not unimpressive in the human sciences, Sternberg et al.'s (1995) point is well taken that there are conceptual and psychometric limitations in the traditional model of intelligence.

Sternberg's (1985, 1988, 1990) own triarchic theory of intelligence is emblematic of the view that I characterize in this paper as *multiplex* because it encompasses the assumption of multiple intelligences, including some that presumably operate beyond the verbal or mathematical realm (see also Ceci, 1990; Gardner, 1983). In the remainder of this paper, I will focus on another prominent example of the multiplex view, the theory of multiple intelligences advanced by Howard Gardner (1983, 1993b). Gardner argued against the single general characteristic assumption and used the term *intelligences* to embrace multiple intellectual aptitudes.

After the first full citation of a work with up to six authors, only the first author's surname followed by "et al." ("and others") is used.

Page number of quoted passage.

The statistical symbol for a percentage (%) is used only when it is preceded by a number.

Gardner's Theory of Multiple Intelligences

Gardner's Notion of Intelligence

Gardner (1983) described intelligence as encompassing "the ability to solve problems, or to create products that are valued within one or more cultural settings" (p. x). In spite of this rather broad definition, he went on to argue that not every real-life skill should be considered under the label of *intelligence*. Rather, he maintained that any talent deemed "intellectual" must fit the following eight criteria:

1. The potential must exist to isolate the intelligence by brain damage.

2. Exceptional populations, such as savants, whose members exhibit outstanding but uneven abilities, must provide evidence of the distinctive existence of the particular entity.

3. There must be identifiable core operations—that is, basic information-processing operations that are unique to the particular abilities.

4. There must be a distinctive developmental history—that is, stages through which individuals pass, with individual differences in the ultimate levels of expertise achieved.

5. There should be locatable antecedents (more primitive, less integrated versions) of the intelligence in other species.

6. The intelligence must be open to experimental study, so that predictions of the construct can be subjected to empirical tests.

7. Although no single standardized test can measure the entirety of abilities that are deemed intellectual, standardized tests should provide clues about the intelligence and should predict the performance of some tasks and not others.

8. It must be possible to capture the information content in the intelligence through a symbol system—for example, language or choreographed movements.

Many Kinds of Intelligence

Using these requirements as a base, Gardner argued the importance of studying people within the "normal" range of intelligence, and also of studying

---

Center headings (in upper-case and lowercase letters, and not italicized) are used for major sections, and subheadings (flush left, in italics) are used to subdivide these major sections.

Numbering the eight criteria sets them off for clarity.

Indicates more than one work of Gardner's in 1993, as listed in the references.

those who are gifted or expert in various domains valued by different cultures (see Gardner, 1993a). Gardner further emphasized the importance of studying individuals who have suffered selective brain injuries. Using his list of eight criteria and the research results from four major disciplines (psychology, sociology, anthropology, and biology), Gardner originally proposed the existence of seven intelligences: (a) logical-mathematical, (b) linguistic, (c) spatial, (d) bodily-kinesthetic, (e) musical, (f) intrapersonal, and (g) interpersonal. More recently, he discussed the possibility of still more types of intelligence (Gardner, 1999), although I focus on his original seven types.

Another list, lettered for clarity.

According to Gardner, traditional intelligence, which is language-based and easy to quantify by conventional measures, encompasses *logical-mathematical intelligence* and *linguistic intelligence.* People who are high in logical-mathematical intelligence are identified as skilled in reasoning and computation. Presumably, this skill is also what Frey and Detterman (2004) extracted from the tests they correlated with the SAT. People with keen linguistic skills are good with words and language. Gardner maintained, however, that these two kinds of intelligence represent only part of the picture. Thus, he originally theorized five additional kinds of intelligence.

Spatial intelligence is demonstrated by those who are able to navigate the spatial world with ease. *Bodily-kinesthetic intelligence* is the domain of dancers, athletes, neurosurgeons, and others skilled in carrying and moving their bodies. A person who is *musically intelligent* is talented in discerning themes in music and is sensitive to qualities of melody (e.g., pitch, rhythm, and timbre). The last two intelligences are part of what Gardner termed the "personal intelligences"—that is, the talent to detect various shades of meaning in the emotions, intentions, and behavior of oneself (*intrapersonal intelligence*) and others *(interpersonal intelligence).* Those who are high in intrapersonal intelligence are adept at self-understanding; those who are high in interpersonal intelligence (called

e.g. for exempli gratia ("for example") is used in parentheses.

interpersonal acumen by Rosnow, Skleder, Jaeger, & Rind, 1994) are said to be "people persons" who have a fix on the social and interpersonal landscape.

Independence of Abilities

> **Subheading is flush left and in italics.**

Crucial to Gardner's formulation of multiple intelligences is the assumption that the various "talents" are not necessarily linked. Someone may perform very poorly in one area (e.g., logical-mathematical) and yet perform well in others (e.g., spatial). This discrepancy calls to mind the stereotype of the brilliant but absentminded scientist, who cannot find the car in the parking lot but can describe in intricate detail the workings of atoms, and perhaps of automobiles. Different intelligences can exist and can presumably be measured quite independently of one another, according to Gardner's formulation. Unfortunately, he argued, because logical-mathematical and linguistic intelligences are valued so highly in American education, tests designed to measure a variety of intelligences still rely heavily on mathematical and verbal skills (Gardner, 1991b, 1993b).

In other words, conventional tests of intelligence measure the same intelligences in slightly different, and perhaps trivial, ways. Therefore, it is not surprising that factor-analytic research (e.g., Spearman, 1927) has often demonstrated a correlation among certain abilities (implying the *g* factor), so that individuals who score higher in verbal intelligence tend to score higher than average in reasoning ability. Knowing someone's linguistic intelligence, however, does not necessarily tell us very much about the person's skills with people or music, or in any other realm.

> **Parenthetical observation.**

The independence of abilities is also suggested by the fact that while intelligence tests predict school grades reasonably well, they are far less useful in predicting routine successes outside the school setting. Barring low levels of traditional IQ, managerial skills, for example, may be related much more to the ability to manage oneself and the task completion of others, or to the ability to interpret the actions and intentions of others, than to the ability to score high on a

> **IQ, although an abbreviation, does not need to be spelled out on first use because it is in Webster's.**

standard IQ test or some surrogate measure of academic intelligence (Aditya &

House, 2002; Aditya & Rosnow, 2002; Sternberg, 1988). Sternberg (1988, p. 211)

Page number of quoted passage.

called these extracurricular skills "practical intelligence" (and distinguished them

from academic intelligence), which in this case seems to depend heavily on what

Gardner called the personal intelligences.

Sections continue without a page break.

Two Main Criticisms of Multiplex Theories

Nontraditional Orientation

Most criticisms of multiplex theories appear to rest on the distinction

between intelligence and abilities that have been traditionally characterized as

talent (Walters & Gardner, 1986). For example, Ericsson and Charness (1994)

argued that expert performance does not usually reflect innate abilities and

capacities but is mediated predominantly by physiological adaptations and

complex skills. Gardner's (1995) response was that the issue is not whether

children are born with innate abilities or capacities, but whether a child who has

begun to work in a domain finds a skill and ease in performance that encourage

him or her to persevere in the effort. That most people do not usually think of

performance skills as "intellectual" is a red herring in this debate, a reflection of

our continued attachment to the traditional idea of intelligence, according to

Gardner. Sternberg (1990) reminded us that an individual who has experienced an

injury that causes a loss of bodily-kinesthetic ability is not viewed as "mentally

retarded." I would add that a person who is very low in social skills, but who

scores in the range of normal on IQ tests, is regarded neither as "mentally

retarded" nor as "socially retarded."

In short, Gardner's argument is that all the forms of intelligence he has

proposed may be given equal consideration with the logical-mathematical and

linguistic forms so highly valued in Western cultures (Walters & Gardner, 1986).

As he put it, "When one revisits the psychological variable that has been most

intensively studied, that of psychometric intelligence or *g,* one finds little evidence

Passage in quotes, with source and page number indicated.

to suggest that sheer practice, whether deliberate or not, produces large ultimate differences in performance" (Gardner, 1995, p. 802). Perhaps it is because experts have chosen to consider *g* and the "academic intelligences" more important than the personal intelligences that the term *socially retarded* is not in common use. However, interest in social proclivities appears to be leading to increased attention to the interplay of the personal intelligences and behavior in different situations

Citations are listed in alphabetical order by first authors' surnames and then by second authors' surnames.

(Aditya & House, 2002; Aditya & Rosnow, 2002; Sternberg, 1997), such as predicting success in executive positions in organizations.

Structure and Amenability to Operationalization and Assessment

  Another criticism of multiplex theories of intelligence is that, in view of their seemingly amorphous nature, there would appear to be unlimited possibilities of adding to the number of intelligences. In fact, as I noted previously, Gardner himself raised the possibility of more than seven intelligences and considers the original seven "working hypotheses" that are fully amenable to revision after further investigation (Walters & Gardner, 1986). For example, he alluded to the "naturalist intelligence" of a Charles Darwin and the "existential intelligence" of a postmodern philosopher (Gardner, 1999). With all these additions, I wonder whether they might eventually be psychometrically reduced to general types, an idea that ironically implies returning to the classical idea of general and specific factors. However, whether the second criticism is perceived as reasonable or not depends on one's willingness to regard intelligence as even more inclusive of human talents than it is now.

  Also, it has been argued that the standard psychometric approach has the distinct advantage of being more amenable to testing and measurement than is Gardner's theory of multiple intelligences. Gardner, on the other hand, has contended that his seven intelligences are measurable but that conventional tests are inadequate for the job. He has proposed measurements that are more closely linked to what people do in their daily lives—inside and outside academic settings.

For example, in applying his theory to education, Gardner (1991a, 1993b) reported assessing children's intelligences by studying their school compositions, choice of activities, performance in athletic events, and other aspects of their behavior and cognitive processes. Although this approach is certainly more difficult and complex than the old approach, such measurements are essential from the standpoint of Gardner's theory, and indeed similar progress has been reported by some investigators in replicating the existence of different levels of interpersonal acumen (Aditya & House, 2002; Aditya & Rosnow, 2002; Rosnow et al., 1994).

Conclusions

The conclusions wrap up the discussion, reviewing the objective of the paper first.

The challenge remains to develop innovative ways (however complex and nontraditional) to measure all the different facets of intelligence (Gardner, Kornhaber, & Wake, 1996; Neisser et al., 1996; Sternberg, 1992). I have concentrated on Gardner's theory as one important example of the multiplex vision of intelligence. This theory encompasses traditional aspects but attempts to move our conceptualization of intelligence beyond those boundaries. For example, when Gardner (1983) described a great dancer as "kinesthetically intelligent," he alluded to a skill that Spearman would not have accepted as belonging within the category of intelligence. That Gardner's model is much broader than the traditional model of intelligence is viewed from some perspectives as a problem because the broader the theory, the more difficult it is to disconfirm. In my literature search, however, I discerned a trend toward broad, interdisciplinary formulations and definitions of intelligence or, as Sternberg (1997) conceptualized them, whatever mental abilities are necessary to enable persons to shape and adapt to their environment. With this broader approach, some researchers are focusing on ways of assessing and improving performance skills that in the past were ignored or considered far less significant than academic intelligence (e.g., Aditya & House, 2002; Gardner, 1991b; Gardner et al., 1996; Sternberg, Torff, & Grigorenko, 1998).

The student gives his own impressions of trends and future directions.

The references begin on a new page.

Perspectives on Intelligence   13

References

Authors' names are inverted, but the editors of the book in which this article appears are not inverted names.

Page numbers of this article or chapter.

Article in newsletter paginated by issue.

Editors.

Capitalize proper nouns in the title.

Capitalize the first word of the title and the subtitle.

Aditya, R. N., & House, R. J. (2002). Interpersonal acumen and leadership across cultures: Pointers from the GLOBE study. In R. E. Riggio, S. E. Murphy, & F. J. Pirozzolo (Eds.), *Multiple intelligences and leadership* (pp. 215-240). Mahwah, NJ: Erlbaum.

Aditya, R. N., & Rosnow, R. L. (2002). Executive intelligence and interpersonal acumen: A conceptual framework. In B. Pattanayak & V. Gupta (Eds.), *Creating performing organizations: International perspectives for Indian management* (pp. 225-246). New Delhi: Response/Sage.

Benjamin, L. T., Jr. (2004). Meet me at the fair: A centennial retrospective of psychology at the 1904 St. Louis World's Fair. *APS Observer, 17*(7), 9-12.

Ceci, S. J. (1990). *On intelligence...more or less: A bioecological treatise on intellectual development.* Englewood Cliffs, NJ: Prentice Hall.

Ceci, S. J., & Liker, J. (1986). Academic and nonacademic intelligence: An experimental separation. In R. J. Sternberg & R. Wagner (Eds.), *Practical intelligence: Origins of competence in the everyday world* (pp. 119-142). New York: Cambridge University Press.

Ericsson, K. A., & Charness, N. (1994). Expert performance: Its structure and acquisition. *American Psychologist, 49,* 725-747.

Frey, M. C., & Detterman, D. K. (2004). Scholastic assessment or *g*? The relationship between the Scholastic Assessment Test and general cognitive ability. *Psychological Science, 15,* 373-378.

Gardner, H. (1983). *Frames of mind: The theory of multiple intelligences.* New York: Basic Books.

Gardner, H. (1985). *The mind's new science.* New York: Basic Books.

Gardner, H. (1991a). Assessment in context: The alternative to standardized testing. In B. R. Gifford & M. C. O'Connor (Eds.), *Changing assessments: Alternative views of aptitude, achievement and instruction* (pp. 77-119). Boston: Kluwer.

Gardner, H. (1991b). *The unschooled mind: How children think and how schools should teach.* New York: Basic Books.

Gardner, H. (1993a). *Creating minds: An anatomy of creativity seen through the lives of Freud, Einstein, Picasso, Stravinsky, Eliot, Graham, and Ghandi.* New York: Basic Books.

Gardner, H. (1993b). *Multiple intelligences: The theory in practice.* New York: Basic Books.

Gardner, H. (1995). Why would anyone become an expert? *American Psychologist, 50,* 802-803.

Gardner, H. (1999). *Intelligence reframed: Multiple intelligences for the 21st century.* New York: Basic Books.

Gardner, H., Kornhaber, M. L., & Wake, W. K. (1996). *Intelligence: Multiple perspective.* Ft. Worth, TX: Harcourt Brace.

Gilbert, H. B. (1971). Intelligence tests. In L. C. Deighton (Ed.), *The encyclopedia of education* (Vol. 5, pp. 128-135). New York: Macmillan and Free Press.

Guilford, J. P. (1967). *The nature of intelligence.* New York: McGraw-Hill.

Herrnstein, R. J., & Murray, C. (1994). *The bell curve: Intelligence and class structure in American life.* New York: Free Press.

Jensen, A. R. (1969). How much can we boost IQ and scholastic achievement? *Harvard Educational Review, 39,* 1-123.

Levy, J. (1974). Cerebral asymmetries as manifested in split-brain man. In M. Kinsbourne & W. L. Smith (Eds.), *Hemispheric disconnection and cerebral function* (pp. 165-183). Springfield, IL: Charles C Thomas.

Neisser, U., Boodoo, G., Bouchard, T. J., Jr., Boykin, A. W., Brody, N., Ceci, S. J., et al. (1996). Intelligence: Knowns and unknowns. *American Psychologist, 51,* 77-101.

Reed, T. E., & Jensen, A. R. (1992). Conduction velocity in a brain nerve pathway of normal adult correlates with intelligence. *Intelligence, 16,* 259-272.

Two or more works by the same author in the same year are designated a, b, c, etc.

Proper names in title are capitalized.

Journal volume is italicized.

Article in an encyclopedia.

Volume and page numbers in an edited series of volumes.

Article with 11 authors.

Italicize the volume number of a journal, but not page numbers of an article.

Perspectives on Intelligence   15

Rosenthal, R. (1990). How are we doing in soft psychology? *American Psychologist, 45,* 775-777.

Rosnow, R. L., Skleder, A. A., Jaeger, M. E., & Rind, B. (1994). Intelligence and the epistemics of interpersonal acumen: Testing some implications of Gardner's theory. *Intelligence, 19,* 93-116.

Siegler, R. S., & Richards, D. D. (1982). The development of intelligence. In R. J. Sternberg (Ed.), *Handbook of human intelligence* (pp. 897-971). New York: Cambridge University Press.

Spearman, C. (1927). *The abilities of man.* New York: Macmillan.

Sternberg, R. J. (1985). *Beyond IQ: A triarchic theory of human intelligence.* New York: Cambridge University Press.

Sternberg, R. J. (1988). *The triarchic mind: A new theory of human intelligence.* New York: Viking.

Sternberg, R. J. (1990). *Metaphors of mind: A new theory of human intelligence.* New York: Cambridge University Press.

Sternberg, R. J. (1992). Ability tests, measurements, and markets. *Journal of Educational Psychology, 84,* 134-140.

Sternberg, R. J. (1997). The concept of intelligence and its role in lifelong learning and success. *American Psychologist, 52,* 1030-1037.

Sternberg, R. J., & Berg, C. A. (1986). Definitions of intelligence: A comparison of the 1921 and 1986 symposia. In R. J. Sternberg & D. K. Detterman (Eds.), *What is intelligence? Contemporary viewpoints on its nature and definition* (pp. 155-162). Norwood, NJ: Ablex.

Sternberg, R. J., Torff, B., & Grigorenko, E. L. (1998). Teaching triarchially improves school achievement. *Journal of Educational Psychology, 90,* 374-384.

Sternberg, R. J., Wagner, R. K., Williams, W. M., & Horvath, J. A. (1995). Testing common sense. *American Psychologist, 50,* 912-927.

"Ed." for one editor.

Major cities can be listed without a state abbreviation.

Ampersand (&) before the last author's name.

Article with four authors.

Perspectives on Intelligence   16

Thurstone, L. L. (1938). *Primary mental abilities.* Chicago: University of Chicago Press.

Thurstone, L. L., & Thurstone, T. G. (1941). *Factorial studies of intelligence.* (Psychometric Society Psychometric Monographs No. 2). Chicago: University of Chicago Press.

Walters, J. M., & Gardner, H. (1986). The theory of multiple intelligences: Some issues and answers. In R. J. Sternberg & R. K. Wagner (Eds.), *Practical intelligence: Nature and origins of competence in the everyday world* (pp. 163-181). New York: Cambridge University Press.

Monograph with two authors.

Monograph number in a series.

Index

TO THE OWNER OF THIS BOOK:

We hope that you have found *Writing Papers in Psychology: A Student Guide to Research Reports, Literature Reviews, Proposals, Posters, and Handouts,* Seventh Edition, useful. So that this book can be improved in a future edition, would you take the time to complete this sheet and return it? Thank you.

School and address: _____

_____

Department: _____

Instructor's name: _____

1. What I like most about this book _____

_____

_____

2. What I like least about this book is: _____

_____

_____

3. My general reaction to this book is: _____

_____

_____

4. The name of the course in which I used this book is: _____

_____

5. Were all of the chapters of the book assigned for you to read? _____

   If not, which ones weren't? _____

6. In the space below, or on a separate sheet of paper, please write specific suggestions for improving this book and anything else you'd care to share about your experience in using this book.

_____

_____

FOLD HERE

THOMSON

WADSWORTH ™

FOLD HERE

OPTIONAL:

Your name: _____ Date:_____

May we quote you, either in promotion for *Writing Papers in Psychology: A Student Guide to Research Reports, Literature Reviews, Proposals, Posters, and Handouts,* Seventh Edition, or in future publishing ventures?

Yes:_____ No: _____

Sincerely yours,

Ralph L. Rosnow
Mimi Rosnow